Pixel Land

A DETAILED GUIDE ON HOW TO DESIGN A
FUNCTIONAL USER INTERFACE, EVEN YOUR
GRANDMA COULD USE IT!

Rahul Raman

FIRST PRINTING EDITION, 2023

ISBN: 9798377865667

CONTENTS

DEDICATION

This book is dedicated to the millions of UI designers around the world who work tirelessly to create intuitive, beautiful, and functional user interfaces. Your work plays a vital role in shaping the digital landscape that surrounds us, making technology more accessible and user-friendly for people from all walks of life.

Whether you're designing a website, an app, or any other digital product, your creativity and expertise make it possible for users to navigate complex information and interact with technology in ways that enrich their lives. Your dedication to your craft inspires us all and pushes the boundaries of what is possible in the digital realm.

To every UI designer out there, thank you for all that you do. This book is for you.

FOREWORD

"Design creates culture. Culture shapes values. Values determine the future."

Robert L. Peters

Pixel Land is a journey through the history, psychology, and important elements of UI design, and it is a journey that you, the reader, will not want to miss. Written by Rahul Raman, a valuable designer and researcher, this book takes you on a journey through the evolution of UI design and its impact on the way we interact with technology today.

We live in a digital age where technology is constantly evolving and advancing. The way we interact with technology has changed dramatically over the years, and UI design has played a crucial role in this evolution. The user interface is the first point of contact for users with any digital product, and it is essential for designers to understand the history, psychology, and important elements of UI design in order to create effective and user-friendly interfaces.

Pixel Land begins with a brief history of UI design, tracing its origins back to the early days of computers and the first graphical user interfaces. With Rahul's fascinating writing style, the book then delves into the psychological principles that underpin UI design, such as cognitive psychology, perception, and human-computer interaction. Rahul explores how these principles have influenced the development of UI design over the years, and how they continue to shape the way we interact with technology today.

One of the most important elements of UI design is usability. A user-friendly interface is essential for users to be able to interact with technology effectively, and the book explores how usability principles have been applied to UI design over the years. The book also explores the role of aesthetics in UI design, and how designers can use visual design elements to create an engaging and visually appealing user experience.

Another important aspect of UI design is accessibility. The book examines how accessibility considerations have been integrated into UI design, and how designers can create interfaces that are inclusive and accessible to all users, regardless of their abilities.

The book also explores the future of UI design, and how advances in technology such as virtual and augmented reality, artificial intelligence, and voice interfaces will continue to shape the way we interact with technology. The book concludes with a discussion on the importance of user research, and how designers can use research to create effective and user-friendly interfaces.

Pixel Land is a must-read for anyone interested in UI design and the evolution of technology. It is a comprehensive and in-depth exploration of the history, psychology, and important elements of UI design, and it is a journey that you, the reader, will not want to miss. Whether you are a designer, developer, or simply someone interested in the intersection of technology and design, this book is a valuable resource that will deepen your understanding of UI design and its impact on the way we interact with technology today.

I highly recommend Pixel Land to anyone looking to gain a deeper understanding of UI design and its impact on the way we interact with technology today. It is a comprehensive and in-depth exploration of the history, psychology, and important elements of UI design, and it is a journey that you, the reader, will not want to miss.

By Joakim Lindholm, 3rd February

PREFACE

Greetings, designers! Welcome to the wild and wacky world of Pixel Land, where history, psychology, and UI design collide in a dizzying array of pixels and bytes. This book is not your typical dry and boring history lesson or technical manual. Oh no, my friend. This is a journey through the digital landscape, filled with twists and turns, laughs and tears, and a whole lot of pixelated fun.

I must warn you, that this book is not for the faint of heart. It will require you to think, to laugh, and to question everything you thought you knew about the digital world. But fear not! I, Rahul Raman, your humble guide, will be with you every step of the way, cracking jokes, sharing tales of my own adventures, and providing you with all the information you need to navigate this strange and wonderful land.

We'll begin our journey by delving into the history of UI design, exploring the origins of the digital world and the pioneers who paved the way for the technology we use today. Along the way, we'll discover the psychological principles that underlie good UI design and learn how to apply them to our own work.

But this book is not just about the past and the present. We'll also be exploring the future of UI design, imagining the possibilities of virtual and augmented reality, and contemplating the ethical implications of our digital creations.

So, designers, I invite you to join me on this wild and wacky journey through Pixel Land. Together, we'll discover the secrets of the digital world, have a few laughs, and maybe even change the way we think about technology. So, grab your pixelated backpack, and let's get started!

Introduction

This book is for intrepid UI/UX designers out there who spend countless hours staring at screens, trying to create beautiful and functional designs. Whether you're a seasoned pro or a newbie just starting out, this book has something for everyone.

Now, I know what you're thinking. "Another book on UI/UX design? Yawn!" But let me tell you, dear reader, this is not your average design book. This book is chock full of history, psychology, and tips and tricks that will not only help you create better designs, but will also make you a more well-rounded and interesting person. Think of it as a design book with a personality.

First, let's explore the history of design. Did you know that the first graphic user interface (GUI) was developed at Xerox

PARC in the 1970s? Or that the term "UX" was coined by Don Norman in the 1990s? We'll delve into the rich history of design and learn how it has evolved over time.

Next, we'll dive into the psychology of design. Why do certain colors evoke certain emotions? How do users interact with different types of interfaces? We'll explore these questions and more, and learn how to use psychology to create designs that are not only visually appealing, but also user-friendly.

And of course, we'll share plenty of tips and tricks for creating killer designs. We'll cover everything from typography to layout to accessibility, and show you how to take your designs to the next level.

So, whether you're looking to brush up on your design history, understand the psychology of design, or just pick up some handy tips and tricks, Pixel Land has got you covered. Let's dive in and start creating some pixel-perfect designs!

1

— · —

THE GLORIES OF THE INDUS VALLEY CIVILIZATION

Good UI design is like a good joke, it shouldn't need an explanation.

The Indus Valley Civilization, which existed way back in the day around 7000 BCE, was one of the world's earliest urban civilizations. It was located in what is now Pakistan and western India, and it was known for its advanced city planning and engineering. The Indus Valley people-built cities that were laid out in a grid pattern, with streets that were wide and straight, making it easy for their camels to navigate.

They also had a sophisticated system of drainage and sewage, which was a real lifesaver when it came to keeping the streets smelling fresh and clean. Not to mention, they had some pretty fancy technologies for storing and distributing water, which was essential for keeping their crops alive and their citizens hydrated. Overall, the Indus Valley Civilization was pretty impressive, and they definitely knew how to party.

One of the most notable features of the Indus Valley Civilization was the construction of large public structures, such as the Great Bath of Mohenjo-Daro, a structure so grand and glorious, it could only have been built by the Indus Valley Civilization - a bunch of bricklaying, waterproofing, weight-measuring, granary-building geniuses. This magnificent monolith, which we can only assume was used for some kind of ancient, water-based religious hootenanny, was crafted with precision and care, using only the finest materials - like brick, and that gooey, tar-like substance known as bitumen. And let's not forget about those granaries, folks. These ancient agriculturalists knew a thing or two about storing surplus and keeping track of trade with their fancy system of weights and measures. It's like they were the Costco of the ancient world. Impressive, right?

Despite being a highly advanced civilization, the Indus Valley folks were apparently too busy to write anything down. But don't worry, we've got plenty of other ways to learn about them - like by digging up their old stuff and trying to figure out what it was for. Turns out, they didn't have a writing system, but they did make a ton of seals. We're not exactly sure what they were used for, but our best guesses are either trading or religious rituals. And let me tell you, these seals are a real hoot. They've got everything from animals to people to religious symbols. It's like an ancient version of a sticker book.

The Indus Valley Civilization was a real hot shot, you know? They were one of the first to have cities, and they were all like "hey, let's live in one place and be fancy!" They loved their farming, growing all sorts of crops like wheat, barley, peas, and lentils. They even had domesticated animals like cows, sheep, and goats, because who doesn't love a good old-fashioned cow or sheep? And let's not forget their fancy trading with the Mesopotamian and Persian Gulf civilizations. They were like the Wall Street of ancient times.

Well folks, it looks like the party's over for the Indus Valley civilization. Around 1900 BCE, they decided to call it a day and pack up their bags. Scholars have been scratching their heads ever since, trying to figure out why. Some say it was Mother Nature's wrath with droughts and floods a-plenty, while others point the finger at nomadic tribes who just couldn't resist a good invasion.

But hey, let's not dwell on the past. These ancient peeps left behind some serious bragging rights with their fancy city planning, engineering skills, and architecture that still has us in awe today.

The Indus Valley Civilization was a real bunch of city-planning masterminds, let me tell you. They were all about standardization, like making sure all their bricks were the same size. Talk about OCD! And their streets were so neat and orderly, you could play hopscotch on them without tripping over a stray donkey or anything. It was like they had some kind of magic grid system that kept everything in place. But honestly, can you blame them? No one wants a wonky building or a crooked street.

The Indus Valley Civilization was known for their brick-a-riffic building skills. They were the masters of the standardized brick game, creating structures so grand and complex, even a bricklayer would be impressed. They built granaries that could store enough grain to feed a small army, public baths that would make Roman emperors jealous, and multi-story buildings that would make skyscrapers cower in fear. But don't let their brick-tastic creations fool you, these bricks were no ordinary bricks.

They were made from a secret recipe of clay, sand, and other mysterious ingredients, and were fired in a kiln to make them as strong as steel. This allowed the civilization to build structures that were bigger, better, and more brick-tastic than any mud-brick buildings of the past.

The Indus Valley Civilization was not only a masterclass in bricklaying and city planning, but they also knew how to decorate like bosses! They were the Michelangelo of seals and sculptures, if you will. These ancient artisans crafted their masterpieces from materials that would make a modern-day artist green with envy - steatite, faience, and bronze.

These sculptures and seals were not just for show, they were also used for important religious and ceremonial events. And let me tell you, these works of art were a real hoot - featuring images of animals and religious symbols that gave us a peek into the culture and beliefs of this ancient civilization. It's like a history book, but with more pictures of animals and less boring text.

The Indus Valley Civilization was like the ultimate interior designer, leaving behind a treasure trove of decor inspiration that still haunts our Instagram feeds today. Their signature moves. Symmetry and balance! Just look at those perfectly arranged cities and buildings, all lined up like soldiers on parade.

In the world of user experience (UX) and user interface (UI) design, symmetry and balance are like the salt and pepper of design. Without them, your design would be bland and tasteless. But with a sprinkle of symmetry and a dash of balance, your design will be the crème de la crème. For instance, many modern websites and mobile apps use a gr

id-based layout, in which content is arranged in a symmetrical and balanced manner, like a fancy charcuterie board. This can make the interface easier to navigate and understand, like a treasure map leading to the golden information you seek.

Indus Valley design is like that one weird uncle at a family reunion, always showing up uninvited but somehow making everything feel a little more cohesive and consistent. And just like that uncle, Indus Valley design has infiltrated the world of UX/UI design with its love for repeating patterns and motifs. You know, like when you see the same button or icon repeated over and over again, it's like déjà vu but in a good way. Plus, it's like a visual buffet of yumminess, much like the intricate carvings and designs found in Indus Valley buildings and artifacts, which are basically the avocado toast of ancient architecture.

The Indus Valley civilization also placed great emphasis on the use of geometric shapes, particularly circles, squares, and triangles. This can be seen in the use of geometric shapes in modern interface design, such as the use of circles to create buttons and icons, and the use of squares and triangles to create navigation elements. This use of geometric shapes helps to create a sense of order and structure in the interface, making it easy for users to understand and navigate.

Finally, Indus Valley's design is characterized by its use of simple, clean lines and a minimalistic aesthetic. This can be seen in the use of clean, uncluttered layouts in modern interfaces, which helps to create a sense of simplicity and ease of use. Additionally, many modern interfaces use a minimalistic aesthetic, with a focus on typography and simple color palettes, which can help to create a sense of elegance and sophistication.

And that's a wrap, folks! The Indus Valley Civilization has left a lasting impression on the world of design - specifically, on the way we create user interfaces that are both aesthetically pleasing and easy to navigate. They were all about symmetry, balance, and patterns that make your eyes feel like they're on a never-ending rollercoaster ride of delight. And let's not forget the geometric shapes and clean lines that make your design look like a million bucks. You could say they were the OGs of design, and they're still inspiring designers everywhere to create interfaces that are out of this world.

2

PHILOSOPHY OF FENG SHUI

A UI designer's superpower is the ability to make a button look like it's been pressed without actually pressing it.

Feng Shui, oh boy, where do I begin? It's an ancient Chinese philosophy that's been around since the dawn of time (or around 6,000 years ago, whichever comes first). It's all about "wind and water," because apparently, these are the two elements that have the power to make or break our physical and emotional well-being. The goal is to harness and direct the energy, or "qi" (said with a "chee" sound) around us to lead to a healthier, wealthier, and happier life. Basically, it's like a personal energy trainer for your home and work space.

Feng Shui, folks, is like the ultimate interior designer's secret weapon. It's like a black belt in home decorating. We're talking yin and yang, five elements, eight trigrams, and the I Ching all rolled into one fancy shmancy package. The goal? To make your home or office feel like a peaceful sanctuary where the energy flows like a gentle river and your stress levels drop faster than a lead balloon. It's all about finding that sweet spot between nature and human-made spaces so you can live and work in harmony.

Now, let's talk about the big kahuna of Feng Shui - the one, the only, the legendary 'qi'. Now, I know you're thinking, 'What the heck is qi?', but let me tell you, it's the bee's knees of energy flow. It's like the wind in your hair, the blood pumping through your veins, the rhythm in your soul - it's the life force! And the thing is, this mystical energy flow can be either a smooth ride or a bumpy one, depending on how you set up your space. So, Feng Shui experts like myself, we're like the DJs of design - we know how to mix and match the elements to keep that qi flowin' like a river. In short, we create harmony and positivity, and ain't nothing gonna stop us.

Another important principle of Feng Shui is the concept of yin and yang. Yin and yang are two opposing but complementary forces that are present in all things and the natural world. Yin is associated with femininity, darkness, and stillness, while yang is associated with masculinity, light, and movement. In Feng Shui, the balance between yin and yang is considered to be essential for creating a harmonious and balanced environment.

The five elements (wood, fire, earth, metal, and water) are also important aspects of feng shui. Each element is associated with different qualities and characteristics, and the balance and interaction of these elements are believed to have a profound impact on the energy of a space.

For example, the element of wood is associated with growth and expansion, while the element of fire is associated with passion and energy. By understanding the properties of each element and how they interact with one another, feng shui practitioners can design spaces that promote balance and harmony.

The eight trigrams of the I Ching are also an important aspect of Feng Shui. The eight trigrams, each consisting of three lines (broken or solid), represent the eight fundamental principles of the universe: heaven, earth, thunder, water, mountain, wind, fire, and lake. These principles are used to understand the energy of a particular space and how it can be optimized like a pro. Feng shui is not just limited to the design of buildings and homes, but also extends to the design of gardens, landscapes, and even objects in the house.

Feng shui, It's not just for your grandma's living room anymore. We're talking homes, offices, gardens, and even entire cities getting' in on the feng shui game. Imagine a world where architects, designers, and builders are using ancient Chinese wisdom to create spaces that'll make you feel like a zillion buck. Now that's what I call prosperity, health, and happiness all rolled into one!

It is important folks to note that the practice of Feng Shui is a complex and multifaceted one and requires a thorough understanding of the principles. In recent years, the principles of Feng Shui have been applied to the field of user experience (UX) and user interface (UI) design. This is because the principles of Feng Shui can be used to create a more user-friendly and intuitive interface, which can lead to a better user experience with darn good hamburger menus.

Feng Shui is all about balance. And in the wild world of UX/UI design, we gotta keep that balance in check. Think of it like a tightrope walker - you gotta keep all the elements on the screen in line, otherwise it's a free fall into chaos. That's where the grid system comes in - it's like a safety net for your design. And let's not forget about contrasting colors and shapes - they're like the circus clowns of design, they bring the joy and make everything look all fancy-like. So, let's keep it balanced and make sure our designs don't take a nose dive.

Another important principle of Feng Shui is the idea of flow. In UX/UI design, flow refers to the way that the user interacts with the interface. A good flow means that the user can navigate through the interface easily and intuitively, without getting lost or confused. This can be achieved by using clear and consistent navigation, and by providing clear instructions and feedback to the user.

Feng Shui is all about getting rid of the excess junk in your life, and the same principle applies to UI design. Clutter in the digital world is like having a hoarder's paradise on your screen. It's overwhelming, confusing, and makes it hard to find the good stuff (aka the important information). But fear not, my designers! We can banish the clutter with a minimalist approach. Think Marie Kondo for your screens. Let's focus on the essentials and bid adieu to the rest.

Feng Shui ain't just about moving your furniture around, folks! It's also about letting that golden sunshine in. In the world of UX/UI design, we like to think of natural light as the ultimate party crasher. It crashes in, uninvited but always welcome, and suddenly your interface is lit up like a Vegas casino. And just like a Vegas casino, you want to make sure you're dressed to impress. So, we use light colors and materials that reflect like a mirror ball, making everything sparkle and shine but not too much. In short, natural light is the life of the party for your interface.

The last addition to these principles, Feng Shui also emphasizes the importance of color. In UX/UI design, color can be used to create a specific mood or atmosphere. For example, warm colors such as red and orange can create a sense of energy and excitement, while cool colors such as blue and green can create a sense of calm and tranquility.

3

THE GREAT EGYPTIANS

Design is like a magic trick, it's all about creating the illusion of simplicity.

Step back in time to the land of pharaohs and pyramids, where 3,000 years of history unfold before your very eyes. It all started way back in 3150 BCE, when the world was still in its diapers, and the ancient Egyptians were just getting their civilization off the ground. Fast forward to 332 BCE, when Alexander the Great waltzed in and put an end to the pharaonic era. But don't worry, the legacy of those impressive pyramids and mysterious hieroglyphs lives on.

Back in the day, Egypt was run by a bunch of bossy pharaohs who thought they were hot stuff. They built big ol' monuments like the pyramids and the Sphinx, just to show off. The Old Kingdom was like, 'the good old days' for Egypt. It lasted from around 2686 to 2181 BCE and was full of prosperity and architectural masterpieces. But let's be real, the Great Pyramid of Giza was the real MVP of this time period.

In 2055 BCE, the Middle Kingdom came to reign and boy, did they bring the heat! Centralized government? Check. Cultural achievements? Double check. Pyramids? You betcha! And let's not forget the cherry on top - the first written legal code. Fast forward a few centuries to 1539 BCE and enter the New Kingdom - a time of territorial expansion, monumental structures, and let's be real, some pretty impressive tomb decorating. Think Temple of Amun at Karnak and the oh-so-famous tomb of Tutankhamun.

Designers, let me tell you, the social ladder in ancient Egypt was a doozy. At the tippy-top, you had the all-powerful pharaoh, the ultimate ruler of the land. But don't get too excited, folks, because right below him were the nobles, priests, scribes, and artisans. Basically, if you weren't one of those guys, you were pretty much screwed. The majority of the population were farmers and laborers, so you had some company. And let's not forget about the gods and goddesses, oh boy. They were all up in the Egyptians' business, with religious beliefs and practices playing a central role in their daily lives. Talk about a complicated pantheon, am I right?

They weren't just good at building pyramids (which, let's be real, are pretty impressive), they were also killing it in the art and tech game. These ancient Egyptians were like the MacGyver's of metalworking, pottery, and weaving. And let's talk about their art, they knew how to make a stylized and symbolic human form look fly. But it wasn't just all aesthetics, they were also ahead of their time in medicine and math. Basically, they were the ultimate Renaissance civilization.

Ancient Egypt, the land of pyramids, pharaohs, and hieroglyphics, had a pretty sweet run. But, as all good things must come to an end, so too did this civilization's reign. Unfortunately, a combination of pesky invasions, in-house bickering, and financial woes proved to be the ultimate downfall. But don't shed a tear just yet! The Egyptians left behind a pretty rad legacy in the form of art, structures, and culture that still has people geeking out to this very day.

The Egyptian civilization was one of the most advanced and influential cultures of ancient times. Their design and architecture were a reflection of their beliefs and way of life, and it was characterized by grandeur, symmetry, and an emphasis on religious and funerary themes.

The Egyptians were master builders, and their architectural achievements were impressive. They built massive pyramids, temples, and tombs that still stand today as a testament to their skill and ingenuity. The most iconic of these structures is the Great Pyramid of Giza, and is considered one of the Seven Wonders of the Ancient World. The pyramid, which is made up of more than 2 million stone blocks, was built as a tomb for the pharaoh Khufu and is considered one of the most impressive engineering feats in history.

Temples? Oh yeah, those big ol' monuments the Egyptians built to appease their deities. You know, just in case the gods decided to smite 'em with a plague of locusts or something. Anyways, these temples were basically like giant billboards saying "Hey gods, we love you! Please don't turn us into frogs." And they were usually plopped right in the middle of town, because nothing says "We're serious about our religion" like blocking traffic. But let's be real, these temples were pretty darn impressive. Columns as tall as a skyscraper, carvings so intricate you'd think they were done by a team of ants on acid. But the real showstopper? The Temple of Amun at Karnak. 2,000 years in the making and still standing strong. It's like the ancient Egyptian version of a never-ending construction project.

You know what they say, when in Egypt, do as the pharaohs do - and that includes building a kickass tomb to ensure a smooth ride into the afterlife. Enter the Valley of the Kings, the ultimate VIP lounge for the pharaohs of the New Kingdom. These tombs were cut straight outta rock and decked out with fancy carvings and paintings, like a roadmap for the deceased's journey to the afterlife. Basically, it's like Egypt's version of a luxury hotel, but for the dead.

In addition to these grand structures, the Egyptians also built smaller, more functional buildings such as houses and palaces. These buildings were typically made from mud brick and were designed to be comfortable and functional. The palace of King Amenhotep II at Malkata is a good example of this type of architecture.

Overall, the design and architecture of the Egyptian civilization were a reflection of their beliefs and way of life. It was characterized by grandeur, symmetry, and an emphasis on religious and funerary themes. The structures they built were not only impressive, but they also served a purpose, and they continue to stand as a testament to the skill and ingenuity of the ancient Egyptians. RESPECT!

Egyptians were all about that natural flow. They believed that everything in the universe was like one big happy family, connected and stuff. And you know what? They weren't wrong. Their architecture, art, and design were all about showing off that harmony and balance between humans and Mother Nature. It's like they were saying, 'Nature, we got your back. Let's work together and make some cool stuff.' And that's exactly what they did.

Atum, the god of the universe, was the brains behind it all according to the ancient Egyptians. They were convinced that everything in existence was a reflection of Atum's power and wisdom - like a cosmic funhouse mirror. The sun, moon, and stars were all just Atum showing off his cosmic muscles. And the natural world? Pure Atum wisdom on display. This belief was reflected in their architecture - they built their buildings like giant sundials, aligning them with the stars and the movements of the sun and moon. Basically, they were trying to get as close to Atum's brilliance as possible.

One of the most iconic examples of this belief is the Great Pyramid of Giza, which was built around 2550 BC. The pyramid is aligned with the cardinal points and the movements of the sun and stars, and it is believed to have been built as a symbol of the power and wisdom of the pharaoh who commissioned it. The pyramid was also designed to align with the Nile River, which was seen as the source of life and fertility in ancient Egypt.

The Egyptian design philosophy (yeah, they had philosophy too) also extended to other forms of art and architecture, such as hieroglyphs and frescoes. Hieroglyphs were a form of writing that used pictures to represent ideas and concepts, and they were often used to decorate the walls of temples and tombs. Frescoes were also used to decorate the walls of temples and tombs, and they were often used to depict scenes from Egyptian mythology and history.

Back in ancient Egypt, the design philosophy in fashion was serious business. You see, these pharaohs and their peeps believed that your wardrobe was a direct reflection of your social standing and power. So, they went all out with the bling - gold and precious stones were a must. But it wasn't just about looking fly on the outside. Oh no, they also believed that true beauty came from within and therefore, they slathered on the eyeliner (to protect their eyes from the heat) and piled on the jewelry to bring out their inner Goddess/God. Talk about high maintenance!

The Egyptian design philosophy was rooted in a deep understanding of the natural world and a belief in the interconnectedness of all things. This philosophy was reflected in the way that the ancient Egyptians designed their buildings, art, and clothing, and it continues to influence design and art to this day.

The Egyptian design philosophy is a unique and influential style that has been used in various forms of design, including user experience (UX) and user interface (UI) design. The ancient Egyptians were known for their strong sense of symmetry, balance, and hierarchy, which were reflected in their art, architecture, and hieroglyphs. These principles have been adapted and applied to modern design, particularly in the field of UX/UI design and yeah it still rocks!

Now, time to get serious, folks! The use of symmetry in Egyptian design is evident in their architectural structures, such as the Pyramids of Giza and the Temple of Amun-Ra at Karnak. The symmetry and balance of these structures create a sense of order and stability, which can be applied to modern design to create a clear and organized user interface.

Hierarchy is also a prominent feature of Egyptian design, as seen in their hieroglyphs and artwork. The use of different sizes and styles of hieroglyphs helped to convey different levels of importance and meaning. This principle can be applied to modern design by using different typography, color, and layout to indicate different levels of information, making it easier for users to navigate and find the information they need.

The use of negative space is another key aspect of Egyptian design philosophy. The ancient Egyptians believed that negative space was just as important as positive space, as it helped to create balance and harmony. This principle can be applied to modern design by using negative space to create a sense of simplicity and elegance in a user interface, making it easier for users to focus on important information.

In the end of the Egyptian party, the application of Egyptian design philosophy in UX/UI design can bring a sense of balance, hierarchy, and simplicity to the user interface, making it more visually appealing and user-friendly. The principles of symmetry, hierarchy, and negative space that were used by the ancient Egyptians can be adapted and applied to modern design to create a clear, organized, and aesthetically pleasing user interface.

4

— · —

THE GREEKS

Art is like a mirror, but with better lighting and a filter.

The 500 BC was the year the ancient Greeks finally woke up and realized that ergonomics was a thing! Like, who knew that studying how our bodies interact with our environment was so important? I mean, it's kind of a no-brainer when you think about it, but apparently it took a hot minute for the Greeks to catch on. But once they did, BAM! Ergonomics became the hot topic of the day. Suddenly everyone was all like "let's make art and buildings that don't give us back pain!" and "let's think about how we sit in chairs!" It was a real game-changer, folks. So, kudos to the ancient Greeks for finally figuring it out.

Back in the day, the ancient Greeks were all about shaking things up. They were all like "traditional beliefs? Psh..., we've outgrown those. Let's explore new ways of understanding the world around us." And with that mindset, they dove headfirst into studying the human body and how it interacts with its surroundings. It was like a renaissance of the body and brain. They were all like "hey, let's take a closer look at this vessel we call a body and see what makes it tick." It was a wild time to be alive, let me tell you.

Now, ladies and gentlemen, allow me to introduce you to the OG ergonomics expert - none other than the esteemed physician, Hippocrates. This ancient Greek was way ahead of his time in understanding the human body as a complex machine that required observation and experimentation to comprehend and treat. He had the smarts to recognize that the body is a symphony of organs and muscles that must be in harmony for ultimate wellness. But let's not forget the external factors, folks - Hippocrates knew that diet and exercise, as well as the environment, play crucial roles in maintaining this delicate equilibrium.

Aristotle - the man who took Hippocrates' concepts and kicked them up a notch. This philosopher was convinced that the body and mind were like two peas in a pod, with the body being the trusty instrument of the mind. But that's not all, folks! He believed that with proper training, the mind could exert its dominance over the body. But wait, there's more! Aristotle also recognized the importance of the environment in shaping both the mind and body. He believed that a healthy and comfortable environment was crucial for optimal development. So, in short, Aristotle was a man who understood the importance of both a strong mind and a comfortable lifestyle. So, if you want to be like Aristotle, work on your mind and make sure you're surrounded by comfort.

In ancient Greece, there was a man of great wisdom and intellect by the name of Pythagoras. Not only was he a philosopher and mathematician, but he also dabbled in the field of ergonomics. He firmly believed that the human body was a miniature version of the universe and that the laws of mathematics and physics were just as applicable to our physical form as they were to the vast expanse of space. Pythagoras viewed the body as a complex network of ratios and proportions that, when in balance, led to optimal health and well-being. He believed that by understanding and aligning with these mathematical principles, one could achieve a harmonious relationship between the body and the universe.

Let me further tell you about the ancient Greeks and their wild obsession with ergonomics. These brilliant minds believed that the human body was the ultimate ruler of all things, including art and architecture. Can you imagine? They were convinced that if a building or sculpture didn't accommodate the human form, it was just plain ol' ugly. And so, they came up with this fancy concept called the "golden ratio." It's like a secret formula for aesthetic pleasure and comfort.

These clever Greeks used this ratio in all their buildings and sculptures, like the Parthenon in Athens. I mean, who wouldn't want to feel like a Greek god or goddess while strolling through an ancient temple? The ancient Greeks knew how to party.

The ancient Greeks were killin' the ergonomic design game. They were known for their snazzy, functional designs that were both a feast for the eyes and a breeze for the body. They were all about the ergonomics, which is basically the science of how people and their surroundings get along. The ancient Greeks were all about making sure folks could move and work like a boss, without any discomfort or strain. In short, they were the ultimate ergonomic wizards of their time.

It's time for Greek's ultimate lounge machine, the Kline. This bad boy was not just any ordinary couch, it was a work of ergonomic art. The Kline was designed with comfort and support in mind, boasting a curvaceous shape that hugged the human body like a long-lost lover. But wait, it gets better. This couch had an adjustable feature that allowed for different sections to be raised or lowered, providing personalized support for various body parts. Talk about a tailor-made lounging experience. But the Kline wasn't just practical, it was also a visual feast. Intricate carvings and decorations adorned the piece, reflecting the Greek's love for beauty and art. So, the next time you recline and dine, remember the Kline and its impressive design.

Alright, it's time to say hi to the granddaddy of democracy-the Kleroterion. This fancy little gadget was used by the ancient Greeks to randomly select citizens for public office, and let me tell you, it was a real game-changer. The design of this beauty was nothing short of genius. It was user-friendly and easy to understand, with a mechanism so simple, even a caveman could use it (no offense to our prehistoric friends). But don't let its simplicity fool you, the Kleroterion was also tamper-proof. It had a locking mechanism so secure; it would make Fort Knox jealous.

This design not only served its practical purpose but also reflected the Greek values of democracy and fairness. In other words, it was the ultimate combination of form and function Now, when you're casting your vote, remember the Kleroterion, the device that started it all.

The Parthenon temple, dedicated to the goddess Athena, was built by the ancient Greeks with both beauty and function in mind. And let me tell you, they didn't skimp on either. The Parthenon is a true feast for the eyes, with intricate carvings and sculptures that would make even the most jaded art critic swoon. But don't be fooled by its good looks, this temple is also built like a tank. With a complex system of load-bearing columns, the Parthenon can withstand just about anything Mother Nature throws its way.

The ancient Greeks were also interested in ergonomic design in transportation. They were known for their innovative designs for ships and chariots. The Trireme, for example, was a type of ship that was designed to be fast and maneuverable. The Trireme had a sleek design that made it easy to navigate through the water. The chariot, on the other hand, was designed to be light and fast, with a simple yet elegant design that made it easy to control.

Designers, prepare to be blown away by the architectural masterpiece that is the Theater of Dionysus. Built in the glorious 5th century BC, this bad boy was the go-to spot for all your entertainment needs. And when I say entertainment, I mean it. This theater could seat up to a whopping 17,000 people. Not only did it have a capacity fit for a king, but it was also built into the side of a hill. Genius, right? This allowed for natural acoustics, making it the ultimate location for performances. And let's not forget about that curved stage, folks. This design feature made sure that every single person in the audience had a clear view of the actors. In other words, no more craning your neck or standing on your toes to see the show. So, if you ever find yourself in ancient Greece, make sure to pay a visit to the Theater of Dionysus. Trust me, you won't regret it.

Sure, the Parthenon and theater of Dionysus are all well and good, but let's not forget about some of the other gems of the era. Take the Agora for instance, a public square that was the hub of all activity - markets, political assemblies, religious ceremonies, you name it. It was the ultimate gathering spot for the citizens of the city and was often surrounded by important buildings like temples, government buildings, and other public spaces.

But the ancient Greeks weren't just experts in public spaces. They also knew a thing or two about designing a comfortable living space. Their houses and other buildings were known for their ergonomic design, with courtyards as the central feature. These courtyards were surrounded by rooms and provided natural light and ventilation, as well as a space for socializing and relaxing. And let's not forget about the colonnades, those rows of columns that created a sense of space and provided shade. Talk about maximizing functionality and aesthetics.

The concept of Greek ergonomics is always around but only recently revealing its secrets to the modern world. You see, it's all about creating products and interfaces that are like a bespoke suit for the human body. Think of it as a designer's version of Goldilocks and the Three Bears - not too big, not too small, but just right. Because let's face it, nobody wants to use a product that feels like trying to put on a clown shoe. Greek ergonomics is all about making the user experience as efficient and comfortable as possible, like a warm hug from your favorite grandma.

Allow me to introduce you to the magnificent concept of "form following function" in Greek ergonomics. It's a principle that's as simple as it is brilliant. The idea being, that when it comes to designing a product or interface, one should focus on the tasks and activities that the user will be performing with said product or interface, and design it accordingly. For instance, when designing a computer mouse, the primary focus should be on ensuring that it fits comfortably in the hand and allows for easy movement, rather than just being pleasing to the eye. Because nobody wants to use a mouse that looks like a work of art but feels like a medieval torture device. Am I right?

Now listen up, folks, because we're about to get real fancy with some Greek ergonomics in UX/UI design. It's all about the visual design principles! You know, the good stuff like color theory, typography, and layout. These elements come together to create an interface that is not only pleasing to the eye, but also easy to navigate. Imagine a world where everything is consistent in color and font, making it a breeze for users to find their way around. And let's not forget about layout, the unsung hero of design. A clear and organized layout means users can find what they need without breaking a sweat.

The ancient Greeks knew what was up when it came to creating things that not only looked good, but felt good too. They understood the importance of balance, proportion, and function in design, and they applied it to everything from buildings to statues to pottery. Fast forward a few millennia and we're still using those principles today in User Experience (UX) and User Interface (UI) design.

When it comes to creating a seamless and intuitive experience for users, designers need to keep in mind the physical and cognitive abilities and limitations of their audience. By applying ergonomic principles, designers can create interfaces that are not only visually appealing, but also easy and comfortable to use. And let's be real, nobody wants to use something that looks good but feels like a nightmare to navigate.

But it's not just about making things look pretty, it's about making them functional too. And that's where the ancient Greeks really had it figured out. They knew that design should not only be visually pleasing, but also functional and comfortable for the user. So, designers take note, the ancient Greeks of 500 BC were truly ahead of their time in their understanding of ergonomics and its application to design.

In today's digital age, ergonomics is more important than ever. With the rise of mobile devices, users are spending more time on screens, and these interfaces must be designed with ergonomic principles in mind. By considering the user's physical and cognitive abilities and limitations, designers can create products that are not only aesthetically pleasing but also comfortable to use for long periods.

In conclusion, the legacy of the ancient Greeks in ergonomics and design will continue to inspire and guide designers for generations to come. So, designers, remember to keep the ancient Greeks in mind when creating your next masterpiece. And users, rest easy knowing that the designers of your favorite apps and websites have ergonomics on their mind.

5

— . —

1900s Frederick Winslow Taylor and the Quest for Workplace Efficiency

A well-designed interface is like a good bartender, always there to serve you up something easy to use.

F rederick Winslow, a brilliant chap lived from 1856 to 1915 and let me tell you, he was a real game-changer. He's the mastermind behind "scientific management" - a fancy way of saying he wanted to make factories run like well-oiled machines. And it worked! His ideas revolutionized the way businesses were run and they still hold the weight today. He's like the Tony Stark of management consulting, minus the Iron Man suit. Without him, we'd still be running factories like it's the dark ages.

Taylor was born in Germantown, Philadelphia in 1856, the fourth of five children. His father, Franklin Taylor, was a prominent lawyer and abolitionist, while his mother, Emily Annette Winslow, came from a wealthy Quaker family.

Taylor's parents were both well-educated and intellectually curious, and they instilled in their children a love of learning and a commitment to social reform.

From a young age, Taylor had a love affair with all thing's machines and mechanics. He was constantly tinkering with tools and building contraptions in his free time, like a mad scientist with a tool belt. But that's not all, folks. Taylor was also a voracious reader, devouring books on science, engineering, and history like they were going out of style. But alas, Taylor's parents had other plans for him. They wanted him to become a lawyer (insert sad trombone sound here). So, they sent him to the Phillips Exeter Academy in New Hampshire to prep for college. But deep down, Taylor knew his true calling was with the gears, not the gavel.

In 1874, Taylor sauntered into Harvard University with stars in his eyes and a head full of dreams. He had heard tales of the great minds that had graced the halls of this prestigious institution and was ready to join their ranks. Little did he know that his journey would be filled with more numbers than he could count, more physics than he could handle, and more engineering than he could ever dream of.

But Taylor was a determined chap, and he set his mind to studying mathematics, physics, and engineering with all the gusto of a man who had just discovered the secret to eternal youth. He was a diligent student, never missing a class, and always taking notes like his life depended on it. But as the days turned into weeks, and the weeks turned into months, Taylor began to feel like something was amiss.

He found the curriculum to be overly theoretical and abstract, and he grew increasingly frustrated with the lack of hands-on experience and practical application. The equations and formulas seemed to be nothing more than a bunch of squiggles and symbols on a page, and Taylor couldn't help but feel like he was wasting his time. He longed for a chance to put his newfound knowledge to the test, to build something, to create something, to make something that would change the world.

However, it was not to be, and after two long years of studying and struggling, Taylor made the difficult decision to drop out of Harvard and return to his hometown of Philadelphia. He took a job as an apprentice machinist at the Midvale Steel Company, where he finally got the hands-on experience, he had been craving. And as he worked with his hands, his mind began to see the beauty in the squiggles and symbols that had once seemed so meaningless. He realized that learning is not about the destination, but the journey, and that sometimes the best lessons are learned outside the classroom.

As Taylor settled into his new gig at Midvale, it became clear that the boy had some serious machining skills. It wasn't long before the powers that be took notice and promoted him to the lofty ranks of foreman. As the new head honcho of steel production, Taylor had the daunting task of managing the machinists and making sure all the parts came out just right. But it didn't take long for him to realize that the factory was a hot mess. There were inefficiencies everywhere, and waste was running rampant. Undeterred, Taylor set out to make changes, experimenting with new ways to boost productivity and slash costs. It was a tall order, but he was determined to make it happen.

This brilliant inventor, visionary and all-around cool dude, revolutionized the production game with his trusty stopwatch and a method he so cleverly coined as 'time-and-motion studies.' You see, Taylor had a knack for finding the kinks in the machinery and the bottlenecks in the production process. He would sneak up on unsuspecting machinists with his trusty stopwatch, timing their every move like a covert operation. And let me tell you, the data he collected was like gold, revealing all the secrets of the production process.

But Taylor didn't stop there, nope! He took all that data and crafted detailed procedures and instructions for each task, turning the machinists into finely tuned, standardized machines themselves. It was a beautiful thing to behold, like watching a symphony of efficiency.

Taylor's methods were like a magic wand for factories every-where, and soon enough, the word of his genius spread like wildfire amongst factory managers and industrialists. In 1881, the Bethlehem Steel Company came knocking on his door, begging him to join them as a consultant.

And who could blame them? Taylor's methods were like a fine wine, they only got better with age. He spent his days at Bethlehem Steel tweaking and perfecting his meth-ods, while moonlighting as a writer, publishing articles and books about his work. In short, Taylor was a one-man fac-tory revolution, and everyone wanted in on the action.

In 1911, Taylor dropped the mic with his magnum opus, "The Principles of Scientific Management." It was like the Bible for managers, a holy grail of efficiency and productivity. This bad boy flew off the shelves and became a best-seller faster than you can say "optimize workflow." People were losing their minds over it, discussing it at dinner parties and book clubs like it was the next Harry Potter. It was the talk of the town and solidified Taylor as a boss in the management game.

Frederick Winslow Taylor's book marked a turning point in the history of industrial management and labor relations.

Before the publication of The Principles of Scientific Man-agement, the management of industrial work was often haphazard and inefficient. Factory managers and supervisors often relied on their own intuition and experience to determine how work should be done, with little attention paid to the scientific principles that could be used to improve performance. This led to a lack of consistency and a lack of productivity, as well as high levels of turnover and absenteeism among workers.

Taylor's book was like a superhero's cape for the world of work. It swooped in and saved the day with its revolutionary idea of "scientific management." This approach was like a detective solving a mystery, but instead of a crime, it was all about finding the most efficient and effective ways to do work. Taylor believed that work was like a giant jigsaw puzzle, and by breaking it down into its individual pieces and studying each one in detail, it was possible to put together the perfect picture of productivity, quality, and cost-effectiveness. It's like finding the missing piece of the puzzle that makes everything else fit perfectly. In short, Taylor's book was a game-changer and a true work of genius.

The age-old debate of planning versus execution. Like a classic love triangle, these two elements must be kept separate in order to truly flourish. Our dear friend Taylor had the brilliant realization that if managers kept their noses out of the actual work and instead focused on analyzing and improving the processes, and if workers were allowed to just do their darn jobs without interruptions, it would lead to a harmonious work environment free from inefficiencies and inconsistencies. It's like a game of rock-paper-scissors, each element has its own important role to play but if they cross paths, chaos ensues.

Another important principle of scientific management was the use of time and motion studies. Our friend Taylor believed that by carefully studying and analyzing the time and motions involved in performing a task, it was possible to identify the most efficient methods for doing it. This would allow managers to optimize the use of resources and improve productivity.

But folks, let's be real here. Scientific management, as pioneered by the one and only Frederick Taylor, may have been revolutionary in its day, but it wasn't without its flaws. Some naysayers argue that it was too strict and lacking in nuance, and that it overlooked the human aspect of work altogether. Others go so far as to say that it caused more stress and burnout for employees than it solved.

But let's not throw the baby out with the bathwater here. The Principles of Scientific Management, Taylor's magnum opus, was a game changer in the world of industrial management and labor relations. And let's be real, it still holds a lot of weight today. The principles of separating planning and execution, using time and motion studies, and worker specialization are still being used in factories, offices, and other workplaces all over the globe. So, while it may have its limitations, we can't deny the impact that Taylor's work has had on the way we work today.

Now on to UX and UI design. You see, these two design elements are like the peanut butter and jelly of digital products. They just go together, like a horse and carriage, or a hotdog and mustard. UX design is all about making sure the user has a magical, mystical experience, like a unicorn ride through a field of rainbows. UI design, on the other hand, is all about making the product look pretty, like a fancy cake with all the toppings. Together, they create a product that's easy to use, intuitive, and efficient, like a self-driving car that also serves lattes. But here's the thing, creating a great user experience and user interface is like trying to balance a spoon on your nose, it's a real challenge. Many designers struggle to find the perfect balance between usability and aesthetics, like trying to make a banana split that's both delicious and healthy. But don't worry, we're all in this together and we'll get through it, like a group of friends trying to escape a haunted house.

Behold the magic of time and motion study! The secret ingredient in the recipe for productivity and efficiency. Our dear friend Taylor believed that by studying the way work is done, we could pinpoint those pesky inefficiencies and give them the boot. But fear not, dear friends, this principle isn't just for factory workers and assembly lines. Oh no, it's also for the fancy-schmancy world of UX and UI design.

Imagine, if you will, conducting user research and usability testing. It's like a detective story where the designer is the detective and the user is the... well, the person being studied. By studying how users interact with a product, designers can identify areas where the user experience could be improved. It's like a game of "I Spy" but with a purpose.

For example, if users are struggling to find a specific feature or are having trouble completing a task, the designer can redesign the interface to make it more intuitive and user-friendly. It's like giving a map to a lost traveler, or a menu to a hungry customer.

So, the next time you're struggling to find that one feature on a website or can't seem to complete a task, remember, it's not you, it's the design. And with the power of time and motion study, we can make it better.

It's time to talk about the big guns of scientific management - work specialization. Our friend Taylor, the mastermind behind this concept, believed that by taking a task and breaking it down into smaller, more manageable chunks, we could increase efficiency and productivity faster than a cheetah on steroids. But what does this mean for us UX and UI designers? Well, it's simple. We take the daunting task of designing an entire interface and break it down into bite-sized pieces, like designing one specific feature or screen at a time. This way, we can focus all of our design genius on one task, producing a high-quality, user-friendly design that will make our users happy as a clam. So, let's all take a page out of Taylor's book and start breaking down our tasks, folks!

Next, ladies and gentlemen, we talk about the granddaddy of management techniques: the oh-so-sexy principle of management by objective. This principle is like a personal trainer for your company's employees - it sets clear and measurable goals for them to achieve, and makes sure they stay on track. In the world of UX and UI design, it's like having a fitness coach for your website or app. Think of it like this: you want to improve the overall usability of your product by, let's say, 10%. So, you set a goal to achieve that, and then you focus on creating a user interface that's so easy to use, even your grandma could navigate it. It's like hitting the gym, but for your digital product. You'll be looking good and feeling great in no time.

In conclusion, the principles of scientific management outlined in our good ol' Taylor's book can be applied to the field of UX and UI design. By conducting user research and usability testing, breaking down the design process into smaller, more manageable tasks, setting clear design goals and objectives, and working to change the way designers think about the user experience, it is possible to create a product that is easy to use, intuitive, and efficient. By applying these principles, designers can create a product that is not only visually pleasing but also user-friendly and efficient.

6

TOYOTA AND THE VALUE OF HUMAN INPUT

Design is like a love story, it's all about finding the perfect balance between form and function.

It's the story of a man with a vision, a dream, and a damn good last name. Kiichiro Toyoda, the man, the myth, the legend, founded Toyota in 1937 and boy, oh boy, did he have some big plans. He started with a small, family-owned business and turned it into a behemoth of an automobile manufacturer, respected and revered by all. But it wasn't easy. This man had to face challenges and obstacles that would make a lesser man cry. But Kiichiro, he persevered. He innovated. He improved. And the result? Well, let's just say that Toyota is now one of the biggest players in the game.

Mr. Toyoda single-handedly revolutionized the textile industry and paved the way for the creation of some of the most beloved cars on the road today. This brilliant engineer was once just a cog in the machine of a textile company, but he had bigger plans. He knew that the technology used to weave fabric could also be used to weave dreams... of four-wheeled vehicles. And so, in 1933, he founded Toyoda Automatic Loom Works, Ltd. and set out on a mission to create the perfect car.

Fast forward to 1936, and the fruits of his labor were finally ready for the world to see - the Type A Engine. This prototype was a game-changer. It had all the makings of a true beauty - sleek design, powerful engine, and most importantly, it worked like a charm. Toyoda knew that this was just the beginning and that his company had the potential to become a major player in the automotive industry. And boy, was he right! Today, the Toyoda name is synonymous with quality and reliability, and we have this visionary engineer to thank for that.

This man, with a vision as clear as crystal and a determination as strong as steel, founded Toyota Motor Co., Ltd. in the year of our lord, 1937. Now, you may be wondering why the company is called Toyota and not Toyoda. Well, my dear friends, Toyoda had a dream to create a vehicle that would be as easy to use as a Sunday morning crossword puzzle, as simple to maintain as a well-oiled machine, and as affordable as a pint of beer at happy hour. And thus, the name Toyota was born. But the story doesn't end there. It gets even better. The company's first production vehicle, the Toyota

AA, was introduced in 1936 and it was a hit with consumers faster than a cheetah catching a gazelle. It was a thing of beauty, a marvel of engineering, and a true testament to Toyoda's vision.

Our beloved car manufacturer was forced to put the brakes on their auto production and shift gears to producing military vehicles and equipment during World War II. It was a tough time for the company, but they soldiered on for the greater good. Fast forward to post-war and it was time for Toyota to rev up their engines and get back to making cars. But hold on just a sec, they were met with a few roadblocks. The materials were scarce and the demand for cars was as low as a flat tire. It was a rough patch, but Toyota persevered and kept on truckin'.

Now, where do I even begin with the Toyota Crown? It's like the little engine that could rock, but with four wheels and a whole lot of determination. You see, back in the day, Toyota had its fair share of obstacles. It was like trying to climb Mount Everest in flip flops. But, like any true champion, they didn't let that stop them. No sir!

In 1955, Toyota pulled a rabbit out of its hat and introduced the Crown. This car was the first Toyota vehicle to be exported to the United States and let me tell you, it was a game changer. It was like the first time someone put pineapple on a pizza, it was just meant to be. This was a major milestone for Toyota, like finally getting a hole-in-one after years of trying. It marked the beginning of Toyota's expansion into the global market and let me tell you, they haven't looked back since.

In the swinging '60s, Toyota was on a roll. They were introducing all sorts of new models left and right, but none quite as groovy as the Toyota Corolla. This little number quickly became the most popular car on the planet, and it's not hard to see why. It had all the bells and whistles. But Toyota wasn't content to just sit back and cruise on the success of the Corolla. They were always looking for the next big thing. They were always on the cutting edge, always pushing the boundaries of what was possible. And that's how they ended up developing hybrid vehicles. They were ahead of their time, man. They really were.

In the groovy decade of the 1970s, Toyota had a little hiccup when the oil crisis hit like a bad case of disco fever. Consumers were turning away from cars faster than a flock of birds fleeing a disco ball. But Toyota, being the innovative bunch that they are, decided to shake things up and keep on truckin'. And in 1997, they unleashed the Toyota Prius upon the world, like a disco ball on wheels. The Prius was the first mass-produced hybrid vehicle, and it was a game changer. It was like putting on platform shoes and bell bottoms on a car, it was that revolutionary. So, while the rest of the auto industry was doing the hustle, Toyota was doing the Electric Slide with the Prius.

Toyota, the global giant of the automotive world, is today spreading its reach to over 150 countries like a boss. But it's not just about dominating the market. Toyota's mission is to save the world (or at least make it a little more sustainable) through their cutting-edge technology and top-notch vehicles. Quality, innovation, and customer satisfaction are the holy trinity of the Toyota empire.

Toyota has always been a company on a mission. A mission to revolutionize the car industry with their cutting-edge innovation and dedication to making vehicles that are as user-friendly as a baby's first toy, as affordable as a discount store knock-off designer bag, and as eco-friendly as a tree-hugging hippie. And let me tell you, they've succeeded in spades. With a legacy of excellence that's as shiny as a brand-new car and a reputation for quality and reliability that's as solid as a rock, Toyota reigns supreme in the car-making world. But they're not content to rest on their laurels. They're constantly pushing the boundaries of what's possible, like a mad scientist in a lab coat, determined to create a sustainable future for all of us. The history of Toyota is a story of never giving up, of perseverance and success, and it serves as a shining example for all of us to follow.

Allow me to introduce you to the almighty Toyota Production System (TPS), a manufacturing methodology so powerful, it's been known to make grown men weep with joy. You see, the geniuses over at Toyota Motor Corporation decided they wanted to make their production process as smooth as butter, so they created TPS, also known as "Lean Manufacturing" or "Just-in-Time (JIT) Production." And, it's a game-changer. Companies all over the world have jumped on the TPS bandwagon, and for good reason. It's like the "best picture" award of manufacturing methodologies - it's won the hearts of many and is considered one of the most successful of all time.

One of the core principles of the TPS is the concept of "Jidoka," which means "automation with a human touch." Think of it like a robot butler that can pour you a glass of wine while you kick back and relax. Except instead of wine, it's all about making sure your factory runs like a well-oiled machine (but with less oil and more human interaction). You see, Jidoka is all about using technology to boost efficiency and streamline production. But, unlike those soulless machines, Jidoka allows for human oversight and interaction. So, if something goes awry (and let's face it, it will), we can quickly identify and correct the problem before it becomes a disaster. And the best part? Jidoka allows for real-time adjustments to the production process. So, if you want to change things up, you can do it on the fly - like a boss.

Another key mind boosting principle of the TPS is "Just-in-Time" production, which emphasizes the importance of producing only what is needed when it is needed. This helps to reduce waste and increase efficiency by eliminating the need for large inventories of parts and materials. This is achieved by closely monitoring demand and adjusting production accordingly, as well as implementing a system of "Kanban" cards, which signal when additional parts or materials are needed.

The TPS, or Total Production System, is like a well-oiled machine, constantly chugging along with a never-ending thirst for improvement. It's like a personal trainer for your manufacturing process, always pushing you to be better and stronger. But unlike a personal trainer, it doesn't make you do burpees.

Instead, it focuses on the concept of "Kaizen," which is a fancy way of saying "let's always be on the lookout for ways to make things better." Every single employee, from the big boss at the top to the person on the assembly line, is responsible for finding ways to improve the production process. It's like a company-wide scavenger hunt for efficiency and waste reduction.

This creates a culture of constant learning and improvement, which is like a never-ending game of Tetris for your manufacturing process. Just when you think you've got it all figured out, BAM! There's a new way to optimize. It's like a never-ending cycle of productivity and progress, and honestly, it's pretty darn exciting.

The TPS also incorporates the concept of "Genchi Genbutsu," which means "go and see for yourself." This principle emphasizes the importance of understanding the production process firsthand and making decisions based on that understanding, rather than relying on reports or other data. This allows for a more holistic understanding of the production process and helps to identify areas for improvement.

In summary, The Toyota Production System (TPS) has been considered one of the most successful manufacturing methodologies of all time, it is a set of principles and practices designed to increase efficiency and reduce waste while promoting a culture of continuous improvement, teamwork, and collaboration. The TPS has been widely adopted by companies around the world, and its principles and practices can be applied to any industry, not just manufacturing. The TPS is a powerful tool for achieving operational excellence and driving long-term success.

Now this is funny, imagine you're a top executive at Toyota Motor Corporation, sitting in a fancy conference room with sleek white tables and a projector displaying a fancy flowchart. You take a sip of your latte and clear your throat, ready to share the secrets of the universe (or at least, the secrets of manufacturing) with your colleagues. "Ladies and gentlemen," you begin, "let me introduce you to the Toyota Production System, or TPS for short. It's like the secret sauce in our manufacturing process. It's a combination of principles and practices that we've been perfecting for decades, and it's the reason our cars run like well-oiled machines."

You pause for dramatic effect and take another sip of latte. "Some people call it 'Lean Manufacturing,' but we like to think of it as the ultimate weight-loss plan for our production lines. We focus on continuous improvement, eliminating waste, and creating value for our customers. Think of it like a never-ending game of Tetris where we're always trying to fit the right piece in the right place."

You see your colleagues nodding in understanding, and you continue. "But TPS isn't just for manufacturing. It can be applied to any field or industry. Want to know how to design a killer UI/UX design? Let me show you!

In the field of UI/UX design, the TPS philosophy can be applied in several ways to improve the design process and create better products for users. One key aspect of the TPS philosophy is the idea of "Muda," which refers to any activity or process that does not add value for the customer. In the context of UI/UX design, this could mean eliminating unnecessary features or functionality that do not serve the needs of the user. Think about it, how many times have you clicked on a button or navigated to a menu only to find that it leads to nothing but disappointment and confusion? With TPS philosophy, we can ensure that every button, every menu, every feature adds value for the user. And who doesn't want that? A product that's easy to use and provides real value. It's like winning the jackpot at the arcade, except instead of a stuffed animal, you get a happy customer.

Another important aspect of the TPS philosophy is the idea of "Kaizen," which refers to the continuous improvement of processes and products (as I told you before). In the context of UI/UX design, this could mean continually iterating on the design of a product, incorporating user feedback, and testing to improve the user experience.

One specific application of TPS in UI/UX design is the use of "value stream mapping." This is a process of analyzing the entire design process, from the initial concept to the final product, to identify areas of waste and inefficiency. By identifying these areas, designers can make changes to the process that will lead to a more efficient and effective design process.

Another application of TPS in UI/UX design is the use of "Just-in-Time" (JIT) principles. JIT is a manufacturing philosophy that emphasizes the importance of producing items in the exact quantity that is needed when it is needed. In the context of UI/UX design, JIT principles can be applied by creating a design process that is responsive to the needs of the user and can quickly pivot to address new requirements or changes in user needs. In addition, TPS principles such as "Pokayoke" (mistake-proofing) and "Jidoka" (automation with a human touch) can be applied in UI/UX design to ensure that the user interface is designed in a way that prevents errors and makes the user's experience as simple and seamless as possible.

And there you have it folks, the Toyota Production System philosophy is like a magical wand for UI/UX designers. It's like a spell that helps us eliminate the ugly, unnecessary, and frustrating parts of design (aka waste) and replaces it with a beautiful, user-friendly, and efficient design that will make you say "wow, this is exactly what I needed!" It's like a secret ingredient that makes our design process smoother than a marble and our products more satisfying than a warm chocolate chip cookie straight out of the oven. In short, it's like a unicorn that takes us to the promised land of UI/UX design. Thank you, Toyota, for this gift of wisdom.

7

— · —

HENRY DREYFUSS AND THE ART OF DESIGNING FOR PEOPLE

Great design is like a roaring Formula 1 engine that makes you feel excited whenever you hear it.

M eet Henry Dreyfuss, the OG of user-centered design. This dude was a visionary in the world of industrial design, and his work still holds up today. He had a simple philosophy: design for the people, by the people. And let me tell you, he took that to heart.

He believed that in order to create truly great products, you had to get inside the heads of the users and understand their needs, wants, and habits. He called it the "Golden Rule of Design" and it's pretty much the foundation of what we now call human-centered design. But Dreyfuss wasn't just about function over form, oh no. He understood that people want to be surrounded by beautiful things too. So, he made sure that his designs were not only practical, but also visually stunning. He was the whole package, folks.

One of Dreyfuss's most famous designs, ah! The Model 500 telephone, a design classic. This beauty was crafted back in the 1930s for Bell Telephone, and boy, did it hit the mark! The Model 500 was a triumph of form meets function - a telephone that was both stylish and user-friendly. Its sleek lines and ergonomic shape made it a joy to hold, while its intuitive design ensured that even Luddites could figure out how to use it. The Model 500 was such a hit that it remained in production for a staggering three decades, proving that good design never goes out of style!

Now get ready to be transported back to the 1950s, when our hero, the legendary designer Henry Dreyfuss, wrote the book that would change the design world forever. That's right, I'm talking about the groundbreaking masterpiece, "Designing for People." This book was a game-changer, a true trailblazer, and... you get the picture. Basically, Dreyfuss wrote this baby to teach designers everywhere about the importance of putting the user first. It's like he was shouting from the rooftops, "Hey designers, don't forget about the people actually using the stuff you make!" And he didn't just stop there, oh no, he went above and beyond, providing practical tips and guidelines to ensure that the end product would be not only functional, but a feast for the eyes too.

Mr. Dreyfuss was the absolute king of his craft and the awards and honors he received during his illustrious career are a testament to that. He was awarded the Presidential Medal of Freedom in 1964, which was like the Oscars of its day, but for designers. Sadly, Dreyfuss passed away in 1972, but his impact on the world of design will never fade. He left us with a treasure trove of amazing designs and his teachings on understanding users in the design process will continue to inspire generations to come.

Dreyfuss, the master of minimalist, has left his mark on the design world like a hot iron on a crisp white shirt. His designs are the epitome of sophistication, yet they still manage to be practical enough for the average joe. He's the king of keeping it simple, but still making it look elegant as all get out. His approach to design is like a breath of fresh air in a stuffy room filled with pretentious designers. He believes that the user should always come first and that by getting inside their heads, he can create products that are not only beautiful, but also usable. So, in other words, he's a designer who designs for the people, not just for his own ego.

His design philosophy centered around the idea that the needs of the user should be at the forefront of every design decision, and that every product should be designed to make the user's life easier and more comfortable.

Dreyfuss had a wicked sense of humor when it came to design, and one of his favorite gags was to flip the script on the typical "humans fit products" mentality. He was all about putting the "human" back in "human-centered design." This meant that every product he created was a love letter to the human form, from the curves of our hands to the way we wiggle our fingers when we're excited. Take the iconic telephone, for instance. Dreyfuss sculpted it into a delightful shape that snuggles into the palm of your hand like a long-lost friend. And the dial? Oh, the dial. It's like he designed it just for people who love to multitask, because it's so easy to use with one hand, you can take a sip of coffee with the other! Talk about ergonomic genius.

Our man Dreyfuss had a unique take on design that would make even the toughest critic crack a smile. He had this brilliant idea of "user-centered design," where the focus was always on the user, not the design itself. Dreyfuss believed that the secret to designing a product that people would actually enjoy using was to get inside their heads and understand their needs and wants.

Now, this wasn't just a wild theory - Dreyfuss put it into practice! He would gather information on users through extensive research and testing, and then use that information to inform the design. It was like he was a mad scientist, experimenting with the perfect formula to create the ultimate user experience. And let me tell you, his experiments paid off

- the results were products that users couldn't get enough of!

He had this wacky notion that design should not only tickle your fancy side, but also make sense. Can you imagine? He was a staunch believer that a product's appearance should be a reflection of what it's supposed to do. He would always say "Form follows function," like it was some sort of magic spell. In other words, he believed that the design of a product should be a love child of beauty and practicality, a harmonious union that makes everyone smile.

And let me tell you, designers, Dreyfuss' design philosophy was like a boss. He approached design like a champion, creating products that were not just pretty to look at, but also super comfortable to use and functional. It was like he had a secret recipe for design success that he cooked up in his design lab.

But the real magic of Dreyfuss' designs is that they've lasted the test of time, becoming timeless classics that still bring a smile to people's faces today. I mean, can you even imagine a world without his designs? It's like a world without sunshine. And that's why Dreyfuss continues to inspire designers from all corners of the world, reminding us that good design is always about putting the needs of the user first.

So, if you're ever feeling lost in the world of design, just remember Dreyfuss' philosophy: design with the user in mind, and make it easy, comfortable, and beautiful. And you too can create designs that stand the test of time and bring joy to people's lives.

Now, it's time to get serious about feedback and testing. Our man Henry Dreyfuss was a firm believer in the power of continual improvement. He'd say, 'Why settle for good enough, when you can be great?' And he's right! Usability testing and user research are like a magic potion for design success. Just imagine, you test, you learn, you improve, rinse and repeat. It's like a never-ending cycle of awesomeness. And the best part? Happy users! That's right, folks. By continually testing our designs, we can make sure the final product is just what the user ordered. No more bland designs, no more unhappy customers. It's time to get our feedback on and make design history!"

In conclusion, folks, if you're looking to create a user experience that's both delightful and efficient, then you need to get familiar with the one and only Henry Dreyfuss! This man had the design game on lock, way back in the day. He was all about putting the user first, making things simple and easy to understand. It's like he knew that people needed designs that wouldn't make their heads spin or leave them feeling like they just ate an entire bag of puzzle pieces.

So, what's the secret to Dreyfuss' success? Well, he believed that visual hierarchy was key, so your eyes would know exactly where to go and what's important. He also thought that feedback was crucial, so the user could know when they've accomplished something, or if they need to try again. And let's not forget the all-important simplicity. Dreyfuss was a firm believer in keeping things simple, so users wouldn't have to take a course in rocket science just to use your product. There you have it folks. If you want to design user experiences that people will love and actually use, then you need to follow in the footsteps of the great Henry Dreyfuss. His philosophy has stood the test of time and is still as relevant today as it was back then.

8

WALT DISNEY, THE FIRST UX DESIGNER

In design, I have two main goals: to keep it simple, silly! And to make it crystal clear. When these two come together, BOOM! Magic happens and beautiful design is born.

Walt Disney was a veritable wizard of whimsy, a grand master of mirth, and a purveyor of pure delight. He wasn't just any ordinary chap. He was a trailblazer, a maverick, a titan of the toon-world. With each whimsical doodle, each animated caper, Walt cast a spell on audiences, forever ensnaring their hearts in a web of wonder. He was a visionary, a mastermind, a beacon of brilliance who singlehandedly revolutionized the art of animation. His legacy lives on, inspiring countless scribes of silliness, sketch artists of satire, and narrators of nonsense to pick up their pencils and bring their own fanciful creations to life.

Disney, the king of childhood dreams and whimsical imagination, was born in the Windy City of Chicago, Illinois in 1901. He was the fourth sibling to join a brood of five, and grew up in a household where the only royalty was the love and hard work of his parents. From the tender age of doodling on napkins, young Disney showcased a flair for art and a knack for spinning tales that would leave his siblings begging for more. He brought his comics and cartoons to life with a flick of his wrist and regaled his captive audience with spellbinding stories and illustrations that would fuel their imaginations for years to come.

Memory warp to the year 1919. Walt Disney packed his bags, said goodbye to his Midwestern roots, and headed west to the land of sun, sand, and... animation? Yup, you heard it right. Walt was determined to make a name for himself in the world of hand-drawn cartoons. He started off as a humble commercial artist, slaving away on advertisements and whatnot, but little did he know, his big break was just around the corner. He stumbled upon a small animation studio that was in desperate need of a new animator, and lucky for them (and us), Walt was ready to step up to the plate. And so began the magic. Walt honed his craft, sharpened his storytelling skills, and before you know it, the rest was history. But hey, let's not get ahead of ourselves, we'll save that for another story.

In 1923, Walt Disney and his bro, Roy, hitched their horses and started a wild west show of their own - a new animation studio! The early days were rough, like a tumbleweed rolling through a dust storm, but little did they know that they were about to change the animation game forever. Walt was a mad scientist in the lab, experimenting with a revolutionary new technique that would shake up the animation world. He called it the "multiplane camera", and it was like a magic carpet that could transport audiences to fantastical worlds with more realistic and detailed backgrounds. It was a game changer, folks! The quality of animation was improved to the point where it felt like you could reach out and touch the characters and their surroundings. This was the birth of Disney magic.

Now, prepare to have your minds blown by the most epic event in the world of animation. It was the year 1928, and the world was about to be changed forever. The legendary Walt Disney Studios unleashed a revolutionary piece of art known as "Steamboat Willie" - the first ever synchronized sound cartoon. And oh boy, was it a doozy! This masterpiece of animation introduced the world to a plucky little mouse named Mickey, who was destined to become a cultural icon. Mickey's first adventure was a huge success, and before we knew it, Disney was on a roll, dishing out classic after classic, including "Fantasia", "Dumbo", "Cinderella", and the enchanting "Sleeping Beauty". It's safe to say, the world has never been the same since.

Disney was always on the hunt for fresh, funky ways to spin tales and tickle the funny bones of audiences everywhere. In the groovy 1950s, the big cheese at Disney decided to take a walk on the wild side and try his hand at making live-action films. But wait, there's more! He was also brewing up something special, a place where people could escape reality and immerse themselves in a world of magic and wonder. That's right folks, Disneyland was born in 1955, and let me tell you, it was a hit straight outta the gate! So much so, that it inspired the creation of other Disney-themed wonderlands around the world, because who doesn't love a good laugh and a touch of magic?

This man was a visionary, a maestro of the entertainment world, and quite frankly, a genius. He single-handedly revolutionized animation and set the bar for all future animators to follow. In fact, if you've ever seen a cartoon and thought, "Wow, that's pretty cool," you have Disney to thank. He was the master of storytelling and his films still bring tears to our eyes, laughter to our bellies, and magic to our hearts. And let's not forget his theme parks, which are the closest thing we have to a real-life fairy tale. Millions of visitors' flock to these magical places to bask in the joy and wonder that is Disney.

Disney's legendary status is a true testament to his unwavering commitment to bringing joy and magic to audiences all over the world. This pioneer of creativity and imagination was a true trailblazer, taking the entertainment industry by storm with his groundbreaking ideas and ground-breaking techniques. With a relentless passion for storytelling, Disney's legacy has continued to inspire generations of aspiring filmmakers, animators, and entertainers. Whether it's through his timeless characters like Mickey Mouse or his innovative use of technology and special effects, Disney's impact on the world of entertainment is undeniable. His legacy will live on forever, reminding us of all of the power of imagination and the limitless potential of the human spirit.

Walt was not just a creator of dreams, but a dreamer himself who never stopped reaching for the stars. He was a man who, with his trusty pen and paper, turned impossible ideas into realities and captured the hearts of millions. His legacy is a dazzling firework display of creativity, vision, and a pinch of madness. He paved the way for animators and entertainers everywhere, and inspired them to never give up on their dreams.

Not only did this wizard of animation cast a spell on audiences with his captivating characters and stories, but he was also a trailblazer in the field of user experience (UX) design. Yup, that's right! Disney didn't just want to entertain folks with his animated adventures, he wanted to transport them to another world, to immerse them in the story, to create a truly unforgettable experience.

Disney knew that to truly captivate an audience, it wasn't enough to just have great characters and stories, it was about the total package. He understood that every aspect of the experience, from the music to the colors to the sound effects, was critical in creating a memorable and enjoyable journey for the audience. And with that, Disney became not just an animation legend, but a UX design guru as well.

Disney's style of storytelling was ahead of its time, and it still continues to inspire animators, storytellers, and UX designers to this day. He created an entire world for his audience, a world where they could escape reality and enter a realm of make-believe. He set the bar for what it means to be a true entertainment master, and his legacy will continue to inspire generations to come. So, sit back, relax, and let the magic of Walt Disney take over your imagination.

His design principles have sent shockwaves through the UI/UX design world, leaving a lasting impact that can still be felt to this day. Let's take a trip down memory lane to the year 1923 when this master of creativity and innovation founded the Walt Disney Company. With his background in animation, Walt brought a whole new level of excitement to the entertainment industry, captivating audiences with his cutting-edge techniques and spellbinding storytelling. And just when we thought he couldn't get any cooler, he took that same magic and sprinkled it all over his theme parks and experiences, giving us the gift of pure joy and wonder.

Disney, being the whimsical wizard of wonderlands, had a secret weapon in their design arsenal: the art of "flow." This mastermind of merriment realized that the key to keeping guests entertained was to guide them through the park like a gentle stream, with no bumps or hiccups along the way. It's like Disney put a spell on the park, making it impossible for guests to get lost or disinterested. How do they do it? Easy peasy! The different areas of the park are connected like a chain of daisies, with pathways so clear you could follow them with your eyes closed. Transitions are as natural as a butterfly flitting from flower to flower, allowing guests to effortlessly float from one attraction to the next. It's like a never-ending journey of joy!

Disney was a firm believer that storytelling was the key to captivating audiences and getting them to feel all the feels. He knew that the heart strings are best pulled through emotional tales and set out to craft experiences that would leave guests feeling like they just went through an emotional rollercoaster. It's clear as day that Disney put a lot of thought into his theme parks, as evidenced by the fact that many of the rides and attractions are built around epic narratives and lovable characters that visitors can get all up in their feels about.

Now, allow me to enlighten you on the magic of UI/UX design, Walt Disney style. Picture this, you're transported into a world of pure enchantment where every click, swipe and tap is a delightful journey. That's right folks, we're talking about an immersive experience that'll have you hooked like a Disney Channel original movie. The secret to this magic, you ask? Well, it's all in the design. By immersing users in an interactive extravaganza, we're not just keeping them entertained, we're building brand loyalty like Mickey and Minnie's love story.

Next up, the seamless flow, a seamless experience that'll have you gliding through the interface like a parade float. No more frustration, no more confusion, just a smooth ride from start to finish. Think of it as the It's a Small World ride, without the annoying song that'll stay in your head for days.

And last but certainly not least, the emotionally engaging UI. This, my friends, is the cherry on top of the Disney sundae. We want users to feel like they're part of the magic kingdom, not just visiting it. By tugging at their heartstrings and creating an emotional connection, we're not just keeping them engaged, we're making them lifelong fans. It's like a Disney movie, once you've fallen in love with the characters, you can never forget them.

In conclusion, folks, let's give a round of applause to the man behind the magic - Walt Disney. His design principles have been cast a spell on the world of UI/UX design and have enchanted designers with their mystical powers. It's like Disney reached into his bag of tricks and pulled out the secret ingredients to create user interfaces that are not just functional but also engage users on a deeper emotional level. He emphasized the importance of immersion, flow, and storytelling, which have become the cornerstone of user experience design. And just like one of Disney's classic tales, his legacy continues to shape the way we interact with technology and digital experiences. So, the next time you find yourself lost in an app or website, just think of Disney's magic and smile knowing his influence is always with us.

9

Xerox, Apple, and the PC Era

Fashion is fickle, my friends. Good design, however, is like a secret handshake between designers - a universal language that transcends trends and fads.

Ah, the tale of the trusty PC - where do I even begin? It's a story that spans only a few decades, but oh boy, what a roller coaster it's been! The first chapter begins in the early 70s, when a group of rebels dared to dream of a world where computers weren't just reserved for big corporations and the government. And thus, the microcomputer was born! No longer would the common folk be relegated to admiring these machines from afar. Nope, now they could have their very own computer to call their own. It was a time of great change, and the world would never be the same.

Step back in time to the days when personal computers were still a twinkle in the eyes of hobbyists and engineers. These pioneers of the digital world had to put their tinkering skills to the test, as they cobbled together their very own computers from kits or built them from the ground up. Picture this, the Altair 8800 and the IMSAI 8080 - two early examples of these groundbreaking machines - were powered by the mighty Intel 8080 microprocessor and boasted a simple text-based interface that was as elegant as it was efficient. These humble machines were the go-to for hobbyists, engineers, and scientists alike, who used them for programming and data analysis like modern-day wizards. It's a wonder how far we've come, but let's not forget where we started!

In 1977, Apple Computer Inc. dropped anchor and introduced the legendary Apple II. It was a scallywag of a computer that set the bar for what a personal computer should be. With its lively color display and user-friendly interface, it quickly became a fan favorite and was used for a broad range of tasks such as education, home accounting, and of course, swashbuckling gaming. Aye, the Apple II was a true pirate of the computer world.

The year was 1981 and the world of computing was about to change forever. Enter the IBM Personal Computer, or as we fondly refer to it, the PC. This little guy was based on an open architecture, meaning it was a free spirit who could be friends with anyone, unlike those closed architecture types. It was powered by the trusty Intel 8088 microprocessor, which we all know is the backbone of the computing world.

The IBM PC was like the cool kid in school, everyone wanted to be friends with it because it was compatible with a wide range of software and peripheral devices. Before you could say "where's my floppy disk?" the IBM PC became the standard for personal computing, solidifying its place in the podiums of computer history.

Back in the glory days of the 80s, the computer market was a wild west show of tech innovations. There were the upstart players like Commodore and Atari, with their flashy personal computers, trying to make a name for themselves. But let's be real, the real king of the computer scene was the IBM PC and its trusty posse of clones. You had the Compaq Portable, looking sleek and sophisticated, and the Tandy 1000, with its rugged and reliable build. These machines were the top dogs, the most popular and powerful computers around. It was like they were the Marlboro Man of the tech world, rough, tough, and ready for action.

Here comes the 1990s. A time of spiky hair, neon clothes, and computers that were the size of small cars. But don't let the fashion fool you, my friend, because this decade brought some serious advancements to the world of technology.

First, let's talk about the CD-ROM drive. This little guy was a game-changer. No longer did we have to deal with floppy disks that could only store a measly 1.44 MB. Now, we could store hundreds of megabytes of information on a single disk!

It was like a dream come true. Imagine being able to play video games, listen to music, and watch movies all on one disk! And the best part? You didn't have to swap out disks every 10 minutes! What a time to be alive.

And then there was the World Wide Web. This was the internet's coming-out party. No longer were we limited to just sending emails and reading news articles. Now, we could buy things online, chat with people from all over the world, and watch cat videos on YouTube! It was like the entire world was at our fingertips. And let's not forget about the endless supply of information that was now available to us. We could research anything and everything, from how to make the perfect grilled cheese sandwich to the history of the Roman Empire.

The 1990s brought us the CD-ROM drive and the World Wide Web, two technological advancements that changed the world as we knew it. And we'll never forget the joy of discovering what these new technologies could do.

Back in the good old days of the 2000s, personal computers were all the rage. But these weren't just any ordinary computers. They were super-duper, turbo-charged machines with multicore processors and lightning-fast Internet connections. These babies were capable of doing things that would make your grandma's computer blush. Want to edit a video like a boss? No problem! Want to play games that would make even the toughest gamer sweat? Piece of cake! Want to conduct scientific experiments that would make Einstein proud? Easy peasy! These computers were the ultimate power tool for all your tech-y needs.

The 2010s! What a decade of technological advancement it was! The introduction of new form factors for personal computers was a game-changer, folks. Suddenly, we were no longer limited to clunky desktop computers or bulky laptops. The world was introduced to the sleek and svelte tablets and smartphones that were taking the tech world by storm! They were all the rage, and soon enough, they became the primary computing devices for many. But hold your horses, folks! Despite their newfound popularity, traditional desktop and laptop computers still remain the top dogs in the world of personal computing. They're the OG form factors, and they're not going down without a fight! In fact, they've evolved to keep up with the times, adapting to the needs of users in various fields. So, long live the trusty desktops and laptops!

Personal computers have taken over the world like a virus, and we can't seem to get enough of them. It's like a love affair that just won't die. These machines have become our trusty sidekicks, following us everywhere we go, from the office to the bathroom (yes, you heard that right!). They are our go-to for everything from sending important emails to binge-watching the latest Netflix series.

But it's not just about entertainment, folks. These machines have revolutionized the way we educate ourselves and communicate with others. Gone are the days of sending letters through the mail, now we can send a message in a matter of seconds. And don't even get me started on how they've changed the way we do business. They have become essential tools for productivity, making it possible for us to work from anywhere with a Wi-Fi connection.

Personal computers have become an integral part of our daily lives, and we can't imagine life without them. They are constantly shaping and defining the world around us, and it's exciting to think about what the future holds for these amazing machines.

Designers, gather around for a tale of a legendary machine that changed the game! In 1981, the Xerox Corporation, the mastermind behind many of our office equipment, decided to venture into the world of personal computers. And what a venture it was! They unleashed the Xerox Star, also known as the Xerox 8010 Information System, onto the market and it was a shockwave of awesomeness. This computer was no ordinary machine. It was a revolutionary device with a mission to bring the office right into your home! Imagine having the power of an entire office at your fingertips! Mind-blowing, right?

Oh, how I adore the Star! It was like a genius baby, born from the loins of the legendary Xerox PARC (Palo Alto Research Center), which, by the way, was a research facility that was birthed by the company in 1970. This hotbed of innovation was a breeding ground for new technologies, specifically those that were aimed at making office work less like pulling teeth and more like a walk in the park. And then, finally, the Star emerged, a fully formed computer that was as easy to use as a slide on a playground. It was designed with a graphical user interface (GUI) that was so advanced, it was like giving a monkey a paintbrush for the first time. The Star was simply head and shoulders above anything else on the market at the time.

This computer was the very first to feature a mouse - imagine that! No more fumbling around with clunky keyboard commands, the mouse was the cherry on top of the GUI (graphical user interface) sundae. With the flick of a wrist, users could effortlessly select items on the screen and navigate the digital landscape like a boss. But wait, there's more! This beauty also came fully equipped with a built-in word processor, spreadsheet and email system. That's right folks, the Star was the ultimate office machine - an all-in-one powerhouse that could handle all your work needs with ease. Simply put, the Star was ahead of its time and paved the way for the personal computing revolution.

The Star was a double whammy of a triumph. It wasn't just a technical feat, but a financial one too. Xerox was like the cool uncle who always brought copiers and printers to the party, but the Star was their debut performance in the personal computer market. It was a brave move, like jumping into a pool full of crocodiles. The personal computer market was just a baby, with the likes of Apple and IBM ruling the roost. But Xerox was ready to take the plunge.

Well folks, let me tell you more about the Star computer. It was a real star, shining bright like a diamond...or at least that's what the early adopters and critics thought. They raved about its usability, packed with features and oh-so-pretty design. But, like all good things, there was a catch. The Star was marketed towards businesses, and let me tell you, it came with a business-sized price tag of $16,595. It was like trying to buy a Mercedes with a bicycle budget. Sorry folks, but this computer was only for the wealthy and extravagant.

With its sleek design, impressive specs, and a price tag that could make even the richest of tech-savvy folks do a double take, it seemed like the Star was destined for greatness. But, alas, it was not meant to be. The market for business computers was limited and price sensitive, and the Star's high price made it a tough sell. Xerox, bless their hearts, had poured all their resources, time, and a good chunk of their savings into the development of this technological marvel, but to their dismay, it was a flop. Sales were few and far between, leading to a significant financial loss for the company. But hey, who says you can't have a good laugh while losing a fortune, right?

Xerox were feeling pretty good about themselves, but then they remembered something important: they were a document management and office equipment company, not a computer manufacturer. So, they hit the brakes on their personal computer market ventures and said farewell to the beloved Star. Yes, it was a bittersweet goodbye, but the Star had to go. But fear not, dear reader, for the computer division was scooped up by the lovely folks at Olivetti. So, you could say that Xerox and Olivetti were meant to be, like macaroni and cheese or gin and tonic. It's all about finding your niche, and Xerox finally found theirs.

Star computer may have been a flop in the commercial world, but it sure made a big splash in the personal computer industry! Its fancy schmancy GUI and mouse navigation were so ahead of its time, it's almost like it was from the future. And guess what? Apple's Macintosh and Microsoft's Windows operating systems just couldn't resist its charms. They both adopted the Star's features and became the rulers of the personal computer market. It's like the Star was a prom king that got snubbed by the popular kids, but ended up influencing the whole school anyway.

Now, the Star was a grand old ship that set sail in the world of tech, but unfortunately, it sank to the bottom of the ocean (financially speaking). But wait! Don't sound the distress signal just yet! This shipwreck led to a strategic change in direction for Xerox. Instead of trying to swim in the shark-infested waters of the personal computer market, they decided to become the suppliers of the technology, licensing it to other companies. In short, they stopped trying to be the king of the seas and became the merchants of the tech world. Smart move, if you ask me!

Xerox PARC, or as we like to call it, the Palo Alto Research Center of Awesomeness, was founded in 1970 by Xerox Corporation. And let me tell you, these guys were no slouches. They had a mission to create new technologies and innovative products and boy, did they deliver! With a focus on computer science and design, Xerox PARC quickly became the leader in the field, leaving all its competitors in the dust. Their work has been nothing short of groundbreaking and has had a profound impact on the world we live in today. From personal computing to the internet to modern design philosophy, Xerox PARC has been there, done that and got the t-shirt.

In the heart of their design philosophy was a belief that even granny could use a computer! Yes, you heard it right, even granny! Their researchers and designers, who were more like mad scientists and artistic geniuses, sought to create products that were so user-friendly, you wouldn't even need a manual. (Who reads those anyway?) And, the best part, they didn't just rely on their own intuition. No, they went full nerd, and consulted psychologists and human-computer interaction experts, who were the real-life versions of Sheldon Cooper from "The Big Bang Theory," to understand the needs and desires of the people who would be using their products. In short, these folks at Xerox PARC were making technology for the people, by the people, and with the people. And that's why we love them.

Did you know that Xerox PARC was the mastermind behind the groundbreaking graphical user interface (GUI)? Yes, you heard that right. No longer were we stuck using confusing command lines to communicate with our computers, oh no! The GUI allowed us to interact with our machines through visually appealing icons and menus that even the technologically challenged could understand. It all started with the Alto; a personal computer developed at Xerox PARC in the 1970s. This machine was a game-changer, as it was the first to sport a mouse and a desktop metaphor, making it as user-friendly as a golden retriever. In simpler terms, the Alto was like a trusty friend that always had your back, guiding you through the digital world with ease.

The Alto was a trailblazer, a trendsetter, and a real game-changer in the computer world. It was the first computer to bring the power of networking to the masses and let users share their resources like never before. With this, the Alto paved the way for collaboration on a scale never seen before. And let's not forget, the Alto's network was the harbinger of the mighty internet we all know and love today! That's right, the Alto's network was the Johnny Appleseed of modern internet, sowing the seeds for the likes of email, file sharing, and remote access.

If you thought the GUI and Alto were impressive, wait until you hear about their other baby steps in technology. Get ready to be blown away by their creation of the world's first laser printer. Yup, you heard it right, folks! It was faster, sleeker and more reliable than its traditional counterparts. Can you imagine the excitement in the office when this bad boy hit the market? No more jams, no more smudged ink, just pure printing perfection. But that's not all folks, they also gave birth to the first commercial Ethernet network, which was a game changer in the world of local area networks (LANs) and, of course, the internet.

Xerox PARC were a bunch of rebels, bucking the traditional design philosophy and saying, "Hold my beer, watch this!" They were convinced that design should be a three-ring circus, juggling the needs of the user, technology, and the environment all at once. But they didn't stop there.These guys were all about the iterative design process, constantly improving and refining their designs based on user testing and rapid prototyping. They were like mad scientists in a design lab, always experimenting and pushing the boundaries of what was possible.

As a professional designer with a flair for humor, I present to you the silly side of the "invisible computer" concept at Xerox PARC.

Imagine a world where technology disappears right before your eyes, like a magic trick. Well, that's what the geniuses at Xerox PARC envisioned with their idea of "the invisible computer." They believed that technology should be so seamless and effortless, that it should be invisible to the user. Can you imagine a computer that you don't even have to look at to use? It's like a ghost in the machine, but instead of haunting, it helps you work (or play!) without any hassle.

This philosophy was a game-changer for user interface design, as it put the focus on simplicity and ease-of-use. It's like the ultimate goal was to create products that you don't have to think twice about - just do. And guess what? This principle still holds true today, as many modern products still adopt this design philosophy.

Did you know that our beloved user experience (UX) design has a secret admirer? It's none other than the infamous Xerox PARC design philosophy! This sultry seducer has been causing quite a stir in the tech world and changing the game on how we interact with technology. You see, this philosophy has a bit of a soft spot for the users and puts them front and center in the design process. Basically, it's all about making sure that technology fits the bill for the people using it. It's like a tailor, making sure the suit fits perfectly.

PARC's design philosophy has been a real game changer in the world of UX design. It's like the LeBron James of design philosophies. Sure, other players may have been on the court before, but PARC brought the game to a whole new level. Its impact can be seen in the way we interact with our devices today. Direct manipulation and metaphors are the norm, and if you've ever used a computer, chances are you've felt the influence of PARC.

These guys were the pioneers of user-centered design, and their focus on testing and feedback has become the cornerstone of the UX design industry. It's like they were ahead of their time, predicting the future of design before it even happened.

But the real MVP of this design philosophy is none other than the Macintosh computer. Designed by a team led by Jef Raskin later Steve Jobs at Apple, the Macintosh was a product of PARC's design philosophy in action. Raskin was a huge fan of PARC's work, and he wanted to create a computer that was so user-friendly, even your grandma could use it. And boy, did he deliver. The Macintosh was the first commercially successful computer with a graphical user interface and a mouse, which were both key elements of PARC's design philosophy.

Other notable examples of PARC's design philosophy in action include the Xerox Star, the first commercial computer to feature a GUI, and the Macintosh operating system, which was heavily influenced by the work of PARC and featured many of the same design principles. Today, PARC continues to push the boundaries of user-centered design, working on a wide range of technologies and products that are designed to meet the needs and expectations of users.

But are we forgetting a major player in design...

It's time for Apple.

Apple Computer Inc. is a giant in the tech world that specializes in the creation of consumer electronics, computer software, and online services that will make your jaw drop. This fantastic company was founded on April Fool's Day, 1976, by a trio of tech geniuses, Steve Jobs, Steve Wozniak, and Ronald Wayne. They say laughter is the best medicine, and Apple Computer Inc. is proof that a good joke can lead to great things! The company is headquartered in the sunny city of Cupertino, California, where the employees are constantly surrounded by inspiration and good vibes.

Back in the day, two tech wizards named Jobs and Wozniak stumbled upon each other while working at the renowned video game company, Atari. It was love at first circuit board! These tech gurus shared a common bond, a burning passion for technology and a wild dream to create their very own computer. And so, in 1975, Wozniak flexed his tech muscles and birthed the Apple I - a personal computer that was like no other. It was packed with all the goodies - a keyboard, a monitor and a microprocessor-infused circuit board. The following year, Jobs and Wozniak decided to go into business together and formed Apple Computer Inc. They hit the road, selling the Apple I to anyone who had a pulse and a love for electronics. Hobbyists and enthusiasts were in for a treat!

Back in the 70s and 80s, personal computers were just starting to make their way into homes, and Apple was one of the companies leading the charge.

Enter the Apple II, the computer that put Apple on the map. This machine was a game-changer in the personal computer market, and it's no wonder why. It was the first personal computer to boast color graphics, and it had an open architecture that allowed users to add their own peripherals and software. It was like the Swiss Army Knife of personal computers, and people couldn't get enough.

In a time when most personal computers were clunky and lacked any real pizzazz, the Apple II was a breath of fresh air. And with its sleek design, powerful capabilities, and user-friendly interface, it quickly became one of the most popular personal computers of the era. It's safe to say that the Apple II was the driving force behind the company's early success, and it helped establish Apple as a major player in the personal computer market.

Apple was on a mission to revolutionize the world of computing and boy, did they deliver! The Macintosh, affectionately known as the Mac, was the first computer to proudly flaunt a graphical user interface, making it the talk of the town. No more fumbling with clunky commands and text-based navigation, the Mac introduced the world to the wondrous world of the mouse and the pull-down menu system. And let's not forget, it was also the first personal computer to strut its stuff with a graphical operating system, developed in-house by the geniuses at Apple, and known as the Macintosh System Software. All in all, the Macintosh paved the way for user-friendly and accessible computing, and for that, we give it a standing ovation!

The 1990s was a trying time for our beloved tech giant, Apple. They were slinking and slithering like a snake trying to avoid the clutches of the fierce competition from other PC manufacturers. But just when all seemed lost, Apple rose like a phoenix from the ashes with the introduction of the iMac. This majestic machine was a vision of color, with a monitor and computer unit all snuggled up in one. It was love at first sight for consumers, who couldn't get enough of its vibrant charm. And just like that, Apple was back in business, soaring to new heights and leaving the competition in the dust. The iMac was indeed the hero Apple needed, and the world was a better place for it.

Now, hold onto your headphones and put down those outdated Walkman's, because in our century, Apple brought us a game-changer in the form of the iconic iPod. This little guy disrupted the music industry and changed the way we boogie down to our favorite tunes forever. But wait, there's more! Apple wasn't done shaking things up just yet. They went ahead and dropped the iPhone, a smartphone with a touchy-feely screen (no more button mashing!) and a camera that could capture all the memories, along with a smorgasbord of apps. And just when we thought they couldn't top themselves, they brought us the iPad, a tablet that combined a giant touch screen and enough processing power to launch a spaceship. Yes, you heard that right, folks! Apple really brought their A-game in the 21st century.

Today, Apple is one of the largest and most valuable companies in the world, with a market capitalization of over $2 trillion. The company continues to innovate with new products and services, such as the Apple Watch, the HomePod, and the Apple Music and Apple TV+ streaming services.

Apple, a company that's always been a trailblazer in the tech industry, has a rich history filled with tales of innovation, out-of-the-box thinking, and an unwavering commitment to creating user-friendly products. It all started with Apple's knack for creating personal computers that even a caveman could use, and from there, the company has continued to drop jaw-dropping products and services that have changed the game. As a result, Apple is now a household name, a global powerhouse, and a source of inspiration for tech enthusiasts and industry players alike. In short, if tech was a superhero movie, Apple would be the hero we all look up to!

Apple's design approach is a delightful blend of simplicity, sophistication, and cutting-edge creativity. It's a philosophy that's been birthed and nurtured within the company's genetic makeup and has been the propellant behind its decades-long triumph. In essence, Apple's design beliefs revolve around the concept that fantastic design isn't just about making pretty things, it's about crafting items that are user-friendly, effortless to operate, and that tackle actual life issues.

Apple's design philosophy is like a beautiful dance between form and function. They've got this obsession with simplicity that's just contagious. It's like they believe the simpler the better, which makes sense because simple is the new black. So, the Apple design team goes through each product with a fine-toothed comb, yanking out every little detail that isn't absolutely essential. They're ruthless, I tell ya! But all this hard work results in products that even your grandma can use without breaking a sweat. I mean, have you seen the sleek lines and clean aesthetics of Apple's products? They're like a Zen Garden for your hands! And don't even get me started on the buttons. These guys know that less is more, so their products usually have just the bare minimum. The interfaces are like a warm hug from your mom, simple and intuitive.

Apple's philosophy is all about making things that are not only super useful but also drop-dead gorgeous. These designers are like mad scientists who are always experimenting with new materials and designs to create products that are just to die for. It's like they're saying, "why settle for boring and functional when you can have both?" And let me tell you, it shows. Every time you hold an Apple product, it's like you're holding a piece of art in your hand. This is design with a purpose, not just to make things look pretty but to make sure they'll last forever and ever, like a love that never dies. And who doesn't love a product that's built to last?

The company is always experimenting with new materials, like using aluminum and glass, to create products that will leave their competitors feeling dizzy and confused. And their obsession with innovation is like a never-ending game of "Can You Top This?" They're constantly trying to outdo themselves, creating products that are not only unique but also solve real-world problems with a flick of their wrist. It's like a superhero saving the day, but with a sleek design and a touch of tech magic.

Now, gather 'round for a tale of the most impressive piece of technology to ever grace our pockets - the almighty iPhone! This little device is the epitome of Apple's design philosophy, which can only be described as a love triangle between simplicity, elegance, and innovation. The iPhone is so sleek, it's like it's on a juice cleanse, and its minimalist design is the equivalent of wearing a bespoke suit to a fancy gala. With its advanced features and functionality, the iPhone is like a superhero in disguise, always ready to save the day with a touch of a button. Our lives will never be the same, and we have Apple's design philosophy to thank for that. It's like a love affair between us and our iPhones, and we just can't get enough.

In conclusion, Apple is like a design wizard, creating products that are not only magical to look at but also easy to use! Their design philosophy is the secret behind their success, and it's all about making products that are beautiful, intuitive, and that solve real problems. The designers at Apple are like knights on a quest, seeking to strip away the unnecessary and focus on the core functionality of their products. And like any great wizard, they push the boundaries of what is possible with their design and technology.

Their design philosophy is the envy of the tech industry, with a reputation for creating products that are sleek, user-friendly, and pretty darn gorgeous! This design wizardry is evident in all of Apple's products, from their legendary iPhone to their powerful MacBook Pro.

Simplicity is key in Apple's design philosophy. Their products are designed with minimalistic interfaces, free of clutter and distractions, making it easy for users to find what they need. This is why the iPhone and iPad have clean, uncluttered layouts that are easy to navigate.

Apple is also famous for their attention to detail. They are like craftsmen, putting a lot of effort into making their products precise and well-made. This is evident in the smooth finishes of their devices, as well as the subtle design elements that make them stand out.

Finally, Apple's design philosophy also focuses on typography and imagery to convey meaning and emotions. Their products feature legible, easy-to-read typefaces, and high-quality images and graphics to communicate information and create visual appeal. All in all, Apple's design philosophy is a winning combination of simplicity, attention to detail, and creativity.

Apple's design philosophy is like the Oprah of UI/UX design. It's all about the user. Apple wants to make sure their users are living their best lives with their products. They want to make sure their users feel like they're on a magic carpet ride of simplicity and ease. With Apple's products, you don't need a degree in rocket science to figure out how to use them. The controls are as easy to understand as a toddler's play dough creations. And the animations! Oh, the animations! They're so smooth, you'll think you're watching a Disney movie. Apple is all about making sure their users get the information they need in a jiffy, like a superhero saving the day.

In short, Apple's design philosophy is a masterclass in making products that are both beautiful and functional. They pay attention to the little details, like the typography and imagery, that make a big impact. They want their users to have a smile on their face every time they use their products. As UI/UX designers, we should all be taking notes from Apple and using their design philosophy to create designs that are user-centered and leave a lasting impression.

Designers, let me introduce you to the mastermind behind the term "User Experience Design," the one and only, Donald Norman! This guy is a rockstar in the world of cognitive science, a wizard in usability engineering, and a guru in design consulting. He's famous for his quirky research on the psychology of everyday things and for revolutionizing the field of human-computer interaction. He's basically like a mad scientist, but instead of creating monsters, he's making our lives easier and more enjoyable when we use technology. How cool is that?!

Norman, the man with a keen eye for both electrical engineering and psychology, was born in the New York City back in 1935. After getting his bachelor's degree from the prestigious MIT, he decided to further his education and become a master of both minds and machines by obtaining his master's and Ph.D. in Psychology from the University of Pennsylvania.

But Norman wasn't satisfied with just being a smarty pants, he wanted to put his skills to the test. So, he became a researcher at the notorious Bell Labs where he got to work on creating computer systems that were so user-friendly, even a caveman could use them. Basically, he was the superhero of human-computer interaction, saving people from their tech frustrations every day.

In the groovy 70s, Norman set sail on a mission to explore the uncharted waters of cognitive psychology. His focus was on how us humans interact with technology and why we sometimes feel like we're fighting a losing battle against our devices. Lo and behold, he discovered that the problems we face with technology are not because our gadgets are evil, but because they were poorly designed. And that's when Norman had a brilliant idea – "user-centered design". This means taking into account the needs, abilities, and limitations of users when designing a product. It's like giving your pirate crew the proper tools they need to succeed on their quest, instead of making them use a fork as a compass.

Norman's journey in the world of psychology led to the birth of his first baby, "The Psychology of Everyday Things" in 1988. This book, famously referred to as "The Design of Everyday Things," quickly became a sensation in the field of human-computer interaction. To this day, it remains a hot topic of discussion and continues to be a go-to resource for all design enthusiasts. In his book, Norman champions the cause of good design, insisting that it should be so simple and straightforward. On the flip side, he cautions against bad design, warning that it could lead to a whole lot of confusion and frustration, similar to trying to solve a Rubik's cube with one hand tied behind your back.

Back in the 90s, Norman was a hotshot professor at the University of California, San Diego. He was the mastermind behind the first ever program in cognitive science and boy, did he rock it! He also co-founded a design consulting firm that was the talk of the town. The Nielsen Norman Group was all about applying the principles of user-centered design to products and services and let me tell you, these guys were the real deal! They were the design gurus of their time, turning everything into a work of art!

Norman, the king of the digital realm, has quite the impressive trophy case. He's been awarded the Benjamin Franklin Medal in Computer and Cognitive Science, making him the smartest guy in the room (at least according to a group of fancy scientists). But that's not all, folks! He's also received the Lifetime Achievement Award from the International Association of Usability Professionals, meaning he's not just smart, but he makes things easy to use too! And if that wasn't enough, Norman was honored with yet another Lifetime Achievement Award from the Interaction Design Association. Basically, Norman is the Mozart of the computer world and his awards are the equivalent of a Grammy.

Norman has left a lasting impact on the way we use technology. He's like a superhero fighting for the rights of tech-challenged folks everywhere. With his user-centered design approach, he's made sure that even grandma can use her tablet without frustration. He's the UX and UI design guru and his ideas and methods are like a magic wand that inspires designers to create products that are so simple, even a caveman could use them. Norman's philosophy is that design is more than just looking pretty, it's about making things easy for people to use. Basically, he's saying that design should be like a warm hug, not a cold slap in the face.

Norman's design philosophy is like a magician's secret. He believes that the best design is like a good illusion, it should be so seamless that users don't even realize it's there! To achieve this, he follows a few simple tricks, like making the interface consistent and predictable. Think of it like putting on your favorite shirt, you know exactly where the buttons are and how it fits. That's consistency. And predictability, well that's like a dance, you know the steps and you can move through the interface with ease. Basically, Norman wants users to feel like they're walking through a well-rehearsed routine and not like they're navigating a maze filled with confusing buttons and dead ends.

Norman has a wild idea for how to disappear into the background and let your designs shine like a unicorn in a field of daisies. You ready? It's all about putting on your detective hat and getting to know the people you're designing for. It's called the 'user-centered' approach, and it's like a love letter to your users. You gotta do some sleuthing, find out what makes them tick, what they want to achieve, and then design an interface that's so perfect for them, they'll feel like they've found their soulmate. It's like a match made in heaven! You can do this through a bunch of fun methods like user research (snooping), usability testing (testing for failure), and user interviews (gossiping). And boom! You'll be creating interfaces so intuitive and easy to use, your users will be singing happily.

Norman's design philosophy has one hilarious aspect that nobody talks about - "affordances." It's like he went around and studied how people use things, and then wrote a book about it! Affordances are like the secret handshake of objects - they tell us how they want to be used. For example, a door knob is like a big, shiny "turn me" sign. It's like, "Hey buddy, I'm a door knob, turn me and let's go on an adventure!" In the world of UX/UI design, affordances are like the neon lights that show users how to play with an interface. For example, a button that looks like it's already been pressed is like a big, flashing "click me" sign. Designers use affordances to make sure users don't have to guess how to use an interface. It's like a safety net for the technologically challenged.

Norman wants you to know about the big deal of "feedback" in design. Picture this, you finally click that shiny "submit" button after filling out a form and boom! The button turns from boring blue to happy green, telling you that your actions have finally paid off. That my friend, is the magic of feedback. It's like a pat on the back for a job well done. Feedback gives users the deeds on what just happened and makes them feel like they've accomplished something. So, if you want to keep your users from feeling lost and confused, you better make sure to sprinkle some feedback fairy dust on your designs!

Good design, according to the almighty Norman, is like a friendly girlfriend. It should be forgiving and recoverable - just like she was when you accidentally called her by your mother's name during the heat of the moment. Forgiving design, my friends, is like a warm hug that says, 'I've got you, even when you mess up'. And recoverable design? Well, that's like the 'undo' button on your computer - giving you a second chance to make it right. Basically, with these two design elements, users won't feel like they're stuck in an abusive relationship with their technology. They'll feel like they're dating a kind and understanding partner, who lets them make mistakes and still supports them through it all. Ain't love grand?

In conclusion, Donald Norman's design philosophy is like the ultimate blueprint for creating interfaces that are cooler than your average avocado toast. By focusing on concepts like invisibility (so users don't even realize they're using an interface), user-centered design (putting the needs of users first), affordances (the things an interface can do), feedback (letting users know what's going on), and forgiving and re-coverable design (not punishing users for making mistakes), designers can create interfaces that are like a warm hug for the brain. The end result? Interfaces that are not only pretty to look at but also make life easier for users, kind of like a superhero in disguise.

10

UNDERSTANDING PEOPLE

Typography is like a musical symphony, it needs to be heard with the ears, touched with the heart, and lived with the soul.

W ell buckle up folks, 'cause we're about to dive into the wild and wacky world of understanding people! Yes, it's a wild and exciting ride, folks, and it all starts with user experience (UX) design. You see, UX designers are like detectives, constantly snooping around trying to figure out what makes their audience tick. It's a never-ending pursuit to uncover the deepest, darkest secrets of human behavior. But why, you might ask? It's all in the name of crafting a user-centered experience that'll knock their socks off! So, these sleuths gather information about people's needs, wants, and quirks, and then use that info to design a product or service that'll have them saying "Whoa, this is just what I needed!

We're gonna learn how to really get to know the people we're designing for, and it's gonna be a blast. First things first, we need to do some user research. Don't be scared, it's not as boring as it sounds. We've got all sorts of options to choose from. We can interview people, ask them to fill out surveys, put them in a room and watch them talk about things in a focus group, or even make them use our designs and see what happens (it's called user testing and it's pretty much the best thing ever). The point of all this is to gather information about our users. We want to know their ages, what they like and dislike, what frustrates them, and what they're trying to achieve. Get ready to have some fun, folks!

Once the research has been thoroughly rummaged through, designers can finally have some fun! They get to create personas, a gang of fictional characters that embody the various user types. These personas serve as the design process's spirit guides, making sure that the final product or service is a perfect fit for its intended audience. Think of them as imaginary friends that help bring your design dreams to life!

If you want to be a top-notch UX designer, you better get ready to slip on some comfy sneakers and walk a mile in someone else's shoes! That's right, folks, it's all about empathy - feeling what the user feels and seeing what they see. It's like having a super power, where you can magically get inside the mind of the people you're designing for. With empathy, you'll be able to craft experiences that are so intuitive and user-friendly, they'll be slapping their forehead and saying, "Why didn't I think of that?

Professional designers like me have an arsenal of tools and techniques that help us to get in the minds of our users. One of these tools is user journey mapping, which is like a wild adventure where designers follow their users' every step, documenting their experiences and unearthing any potential troubles they may face. And then there's usability testing, where designers can sit back and watch their users interact with their product or service like a one-man audience at a live theater show. The only difference is, at the end of the show, designers get feedback on the usability of their product and can make any necessary improvements. Who knew designing could be so much fun!

But, if you want to be a master at creating products and services that people will adore, then you better buckle up for a wild ride! Understanding people is like a never-ending game of whack-a-mole. Just when you think you've got them figured out, BAM! They change their minds. But fear not, with continual testing and analysis of user data, you'll have the power to unlock the secrets of their hearts. You'll know what makes them tick and what makes them go, "meh." It's like being a detective in a mystery movie, only instead of solving crimes, you're solving the mystery of why people are using your product in a certain way.

Now, have you heard of Emotional Design? It's the hot new way to get all up in people's feels. This funky concept is all about how design can make you feel all warm and fuzzy (or cold and prickly, if that's what they're going for). It's a mixture of colors, shapes, and navigation that can make you feel like a kid in a candy store, or a teenager in love for the first time. Emotional Design is the new kid on the block, but it's quickly becoming the belle of the ball, with all the cool companies and designers jumping on board. They're realizing that in order to connect with people, you gotta hit 'em where it hurts, err, I mean where it feels good - in the heart!

Creating an emotionally designed product or experience is like baking a cake with mood sprinkles. You've got to know which emotions you're craving - joy, excitement, relaxation, or calm? It's like deciding what flavor of cake you want - vanilla, chocolate, or strawberry? Then comes the fun part, picking out the design elements that'll make your emotions rise to the top like cream on a delicious cake. It's all about the colors, shapes, patterns, and the overall design that'll make your experience as smooth as a knife cutting through warm butter. Navigation is key too; you don't want to end up lost in a maze of emotions like a rat in a labyrinth.

As a designer, I have a secret weapon in my arsenal - the use of color. It's like a magical fairy dust that can instantly transport your emotions to a different world. Can you imagine a world without colors? Boring, right? That's why color is an important aspect of emotional design. Think of it like this, you want to create an experience that's like a rollercoaster ride of emotions - high and low, fast and slow. And what better way to do that than through the use of color?

For instance, the color red is like a shot of caffeine to your emotions. It's like a red bull that gives you wings, making you feel energetic and lively. On the other hand, blue is like a glass of chamomile tea. It's calming and soothing, and you'll feel as tranquil as a sea breeze. Designers have the power to evoke a specific emotional response from their audience just by selecting the right colors. It's like cooking, you choose the right spices to create the perfect dish. In this case, the dish is the emotional experience.

So, next time you see a design, take a closer look at the colors. It's like a hidden message that the designer wants to convey to you. And who knows, it might just take you on a wild ride of emotions!

Picture this, folks. You're strolling down the street and suddenly you come across a building with round, plushy curves that make you feel like you're being hugged by a giant teddy bear. That's the magic of emotional design, folks! The shapes and forms used in a design have the power to bring out emotions like you wouldn't believe. Take, for instance, those pointy, jagged edges that scream "HEY, pay attention to me!" They'll get your heart racing and your adrenaline pumping in no time. Design isn't just about making things look pretty, it's about making you feel pretty too. That's why designers have to be meticulous when it comes to choosing the shapes and forms they use. Because, in the end, it's all about creating a unique emotional experience for you, the user.

Now, imagine again, walking into a room filled with random furniture, scattered books, and tangled cords - it's like a maze of madness, right? That's exactly how a cluttered and confusing layout feels to a user. It's like trying to navigate through a hoarder's house without a map. On the other hand, have you ever strolled into a Zen Garden? Everything is in its place, there's a clear path, and you just feel at peace. That's the magic of a clean and easy-to-navigate layout. It's like a trip to Disneyland, but instead of Mickey Mouse, you get to experience a flood of positive emotions. Understand these tips designers! You are like wizards, casting spells to create a specific emotional experience for users. With the right layout and navigation, you can make them feel like they're in a magical world of ease and calm.

I have to say that emotional design is not just about making things look pretty, it's about understanding your user's thoughts and feelings and the way they boogie with your product or experience. It's all about knowing what they crave, desire and feel, and how to design the product or experience in such a way that it speaks to their hearts. Just imagine, if you design a website for a financial institution, you want it to make the user feel like their money is safe and secure, like a warm blanket on a chilly winter's night. On the other hand, if you design a website for a social media platform, you want it to be the life of the party, filled with excitement and connection, like a wild dance floor at a funky music festival.

Well folks, let me tell you, understanding people's behavior is a bit like solving a mystery. And just like any good detective, we need to understand the nitty-gritty of the human brain and how it functions. People are like little computers, using different cognitive processes to interact with the world around them, such as perception, memory, and problem-solving. So, imagine if you will, creating interfaces that make sense to the average Joe and Jane. By understanding how people process information and make decisions, designers can create interfaces that are user-friendly and easy to use.

And that's not all, folks! We also need to consider the environment in which people will be using the product or service. Think about it, if you're trying to use your phone while hiking up a mountain, your behavior will be different than if you were sitting on your couch. So, it's important to understand the context in which people will be using the product or service, such as their physical location, the device they are using, and the time of day. With this information, designers can create interfaces that are tailored to their needs and goals, making their user experience a breeze.

People's emotions and attitudes are like a box of chocolates, you never know what you're gonna get. But let's be real, it's all about the chocolate, right? Well, it's the same with people's behavior. Understanding their emotions and attitudes is key to creating a product or service that they'll love as much as they love that chocolate. Just imagine a grumpy person trying to use a product while they're feeling stressed and frustrated. It's like trying to fit a square chocolate in a round hole. But on the other hand, if they're feeling happy and relaxed, using a product is as easy as taking a bite out of a creamy truffle. So, designers, pay attention to people's emotions and attitudes and create interfaces that will bring a smile to their face.

Culture and society play a big role in shaping people's behavior and attitudes. It's like trying different flavors of chocolate from around the world. Each culture has its own unique taste and preferences. For example, some cultures value privacy and security more than others, which can affect how they use a product or service. Designers, please don't make the mistake (like Facebook) of thinking one size fits all. Understand the cultural and societal factors and create interfaces that cater to the diverse tastes of different users.

In conclusion, folks, if you want to create a kick-ass UX design, you gotta understand the people using it! Think about their wants, needs, goals, and what makes them tick. Know their cognitive processes, emotions, and attitudes. Don't forget about the big picture, like cultural and societal factors. With all this info, you can design something that's not just functional, but actually enjoyable to use. Basically, you'll have a design that people will love using, and that's what it's all about.

11

— . —

HOW EMOTION WORKS

Behind every killer design lies an epic tale worthy of a Hollywood blockbuster.

Emotions are like a wild stallion, driving human behavior with a fierce passion! And in the world of UX/UI design, emotions are the secret sauce that makes or breaks a successful digital product. It's like a game of tug-of-war, where designers have to balance the needs and desires of users with their own creative vision. But fear not, folks! By tapping into the power of emotions, designers can create designs that leave users feeling warm, fuzzy, and oh-so-satisfied. So put on your thinking cap, grab a handful of emotions, and let's create some magic!

Emotions ain't just the itchy and scratchy feelings we get from the world around us. Nope, they are powerful forces that shape our very existence! Let me break it down for you, like a giraffe breaking down branches for a snack. When you're trying to navigate a website or app and you start feeling like a wet noodle that's been microwaved, you're gonna say "later, website!" And chances are, you won't be recommending it to your buds either. But on the flip side, when you're using a website or app and it's making you feel like you just won the lottery, you'll be all like, "HELL YEAH, APP! YOU'RE THE BEST!" and you'll be a customer for life, spreading the good word far and wide. Get it? Good.

Now, users may experience a whole range of emotions when interacting with a product - from elation to frustration, excitement to boredom. And it's our job as designers to anticipate and address these feelings.

Take anxiety, for instance. We've all been there, sweating bullets while trying to complete a task on a website or app. But what if I told you, there's a cure for that? Clear labeling, simple language, and progress indicators - these are the tools of our trade. By using them, we can soothe the user's frayed nerves and bring a smile to their face. And who doesn't love a happy customer, right?

It's also about building trust and connection between the user and the product. And let me tell you, it's not rocket science! All you gotta do is make the interface as easy as pie to use and make sure it's consistent across all platforms like a good pair of shoes. You can sprinkle some personalized messages, social connections and let the users do some creative cooking with user-generated content. And voila! You've got a recipe for a sense of community and belonging that'll make everyone feel like they're at a big ol' family reunion.

Now, this is serious business we're talking about here! Emotions are like a rollercoaster, they go up, they go down, they loop the loop and make you feel dizzy. That's why it's crucial for us to stay on top of things and make sure our designs are hitting all the right notes for our users. It's like conducting a symphony, you can't just write the score and call it a day, you gotta test and tweak and adjust until you've got the perfect harmony. User testing is like a concert, where you get to see how your audience reacts to your masterpiece. Surveys are like a choir, where you ask for the opinions of your audience to see if they're all singing from the same hymn sheet. And finally, user feedback is like a musical instrument, you have to listen to it carefully to see if it's in tune or not.

From a biological perspective, our emotions are like a wild party happening in our bodies! Our limbic system is the DJ, whipping up a frenzy of feelings, with the amygdala as the bouncer, making sure fear doesn't get too rowdy. The hippocampus is the designated driver, keeping memories and emotions in check. Meanwhile, the hypothalamus and autonomic nervous system are like the bartenders, making sure we don't get too hot and sweaty by regulating our heart rate and breathing. Understanding all this ruckus can help designers create spaces and products that will evoke the exact emotions they want from us, like making us feel happy, calm, or even a little scared. It's like a roller coaster ride, but for our emotions!

From a psychological perspective, they're like the wild, crazy, and unpredictable creatures of the brain-land. It's all about subjective experiences, you know, like being tickled by the Tooth Fairy or believing in unicorns. And just like a magician, our thoughts, beliefs, and past experiences can influence these emotions to appear or disappear in a puff of smoke.

Now, each emotion is like a different superhero with their own unique powers. For instance, happiness is the life of the party, it's got positive thoughts, a sense of euphoria, and a knack for left prefrontal cortex activities. On the other hand, sadness is the grump of the group, it's all about negative thoughts, hopelessness, and increased activity in the right prefrontal cortex. Just like the dynamic duo, Batman and Robin, these two emotions are always bouncing off each other, creating a never-ending battle of the brain.

Envisage yourself walking into a cozy living room where the walls are painted in warm shades of yellow and orange, the lighting is soft and inviting, and the furniture is all rounded and curved. Feels like a hug, doesn't it? That's the power of design in action! Designers can play with your emotions and create a specific atmosphere just by using certain colors, shapes, patterns, and lighting.

But it's not just about creating a pretty picture. Designers can also use psychology to influence your actions. They can use sneaky little tricks to make you want to buy that expensive handbag or sign up for that new service. They know what makes you tick and how to tap into your desires. It's like the designer is whispering sweet nothings in your ear, and before you know it, you're in love with the product or service!

But seriously folks, the interplay between biology and psychology in design is no joke. It's like a comedic act that brings the house down every time. By tapping into the physiology and psychology of emotions, designers can create designs that will have us rolling in the aisles with laughter, or wiping away tears of joy. It's like a stand-up comedy routine where the designer is the master of ceremonies and we're the audience, eagerly awaiting their next punchline.

And let me tell you, designers are no strangers to punchlines. They use design to hit us right in the feels, to evoke specific emotions and elicit desired responses. It's like a juggling act, where they toss around colors, shapes, and textures to keep us on the edge of our seats. By creating a sense of connection, trust, and engagement through design, they ensure that everyone is having a jolly good time.

So, when you're feeling overwhelmed by a design, just remember, it's all part of the act. The designer is trying to make you feel something, to connect with you on an emotional level. And if they're doing their job right, you'll be laughing, crying, or simply enjoying the show. And isn't that what good design is all about? Bringing a smile to our faces and a chuckle to our hearts.

Now, there's a whole spectrum of feelings we experience on a daily basis. Each one has its own unique personality and quirks, like a bunch of mischievous imps waiting to pounce on us at any moment!

Let's start with happiness, the bubbly and cheerful emotion that makes you feel like you're walking on sunshine! Happiness is triggered by the good stuff in life, like getting a compliment or accomplishing a goal. In the digital realm, happiness can come in the form of a smiley emoji or a "like" on a social media post, like finding a pot of gold at the end of the internet rainbow.

Sadness is the complete opposite, a real downer that can make you feel like the weight of the world is on your shoulders. It's triggered by negative experiences, like losing a loved one or feeling disappointed. In the digital world, sadness can hit you like a truck, when you receive a mean message or see someone else's happy post, like getting a "delete" instead of a "like."

Fear is like a superhero, always there to protect you from danger! It's triggered by the perception of threat or danger, like seeing a spider or hearing a loud noise. In the digital realm, fear can lurk behind every message, like a ninja waiting to attack, with the power to make you tremble with terror.

Anger is like a fire-breathing dragon, always ready to unleash its fury! It's triggered by perceived injustices or wrongdoing, like getting ripped off or witnessing cyber-bullying. In the digital world, anger can be ignited by a biased news story or a misleading headline, like a spark that ignites a raging inferno.

Love is like a warm and fuzzy blanket, always there to comfort you. It's triggered by feelings of affection and attachment towards someone else, like a best friend or a significant other. In the digital world, love can be expressed through a romantic message or a picture of a loved one, like a ray of sunshine on a cloudy day.

These are just few examples of the many different emotions we experience in the digital world. But remember, emotions are like a box of chocolates, you never know what you're going to get! They can be influenced by a whole bunch of factors, like the weather, your mood, and even the phase of the moon.

In the end of the line, to navigate the emotional landscape of digital interactions, it is important to be aware of the emotions that we experience and the triggers that cause them. By understanding our emotions and how they are triggered, we can take steps to manage them healthily and positively, ultimately leading to more fulfilling and meaningful digital interactions.

12

— · —

DANCING WITH INTERACTIONS AND EMOTIONS

Technology may have changed the world, but good design will always make it a better place to live in... unless, of course, you're a toaster.

When it comes to UI design, it's not just about making things look pretty. It's about understanding the way users interact with technology and creating a design that makes sense for them. And this is where the wild world of Interaction Psychology comes into play.

You see, Interaction Psychology is a quirky little discipline that combines elements of psychology, sociology, and technology. It's like a mad scientist's laboratory where designers experiment with user behavior, technology, and design elements to create a user experience that is both intuitive and delightful.

But why is Interaction Psychology so important in UI design? Well, let's put it this way. Imagine you're at a party and you're trying to make a new friend. You might strike up a conversation and ask them questions about their interests, right? Similarly, Interaction Psychology is like the first conversation designers have with users. It helps them understand what users like, what they don't like, and how they interact with technology.

So, let's dive into the world of Interaction Psychology and learn about some of the key elements that make UI design so much fun.

First up, we have the classic "Jedi Mind Trick" technique. No, we're not talking about using the force to manipulate users (although that would be pretty cool). Instead, it's about using subtle cues and nudges to guide users in the direction you want them to go. For example, you might place a "submit" button in a prominent location, or use a bright color to draw attention to an important link.

Next, we have "The Invisible Hand" approach. This is all about making things as intuitive and natural as possible. Designers use this technique to create interfaces that feel like second nature to users, and that they can easily navigate without thinking too much about it. For example, they might use familiar symbols, like a hamburger icon, to represent a menu, or use swipe gestures to navigate between pages.

And then there's the "Surprise and Delight" method. This is all about using small, unexpected touches to delight users and make their experience more memorable. For example, you might include an animated loading icon, or add a fun little sound effect when a user completes a task.

Finally, there's the "What Would You Do?" technique. This is where designers put themselves in the shoes of their users and ask themselves what they would do in a given situation. For example, if you were designing a website for a new restaurant, you might ask yourself what kind of information you would want to know if you were looking for a place to eat. Would you want to know about the menu? The location? The hours of operation? This approach helps designers create interfaces that meet the needs and expectations of their users.

The ultimate goal of interaction psychology is to create digital products that are intuitive and user-friendly. This is where UI design comes in. UI designers use interaction psychology to create interfaces that are easy to use and that feel natural to users.

Let's take a look at an example. Imagine you are designing a to-do list app. The first thing you want to do is make it easy for users to add tasks. You can do this by using interaction psychology. You can place a big, juicy "Add Task" button in a prominent location, and make sure it's easy to tap. This way, users won't have to waste time searching for the add task function.

But hold on a second, you also don't want to overload users with too many options. That's why it's important to keep the design simple and uncluttered. If users are overwhelmed with too many options, they may abandon the app and never come back.

Interaction psychology also plays a role in the design of error messages. Error messages can be frustrating for users, especially if they don't understand what went wrong. To avoid this frustration, designers can use interaction psychology to create error messages that are clear, concise, and easy to understand. For example, instead of just displaying an error code, a UI designer can include a friendly message that explains the problem and suggests how to fix it.

As UI designers, we often get caught up in creating visually appealing designs and forget the importance of understanding user motivation and behavior. The truth is, if we don't understand what motivates our users and how they behave, we can end up with designs that are not only visually unappealing, but also completely useless. Now, we'll dive into the world of user motivation and behavior and explore the different ways we can make our designs more usable, accessible, and enjoyable for our users.

Let's start with a story. Imagine you're at a restaurant and the menu is written in a foreign language. You have no idea what any of the dishes are, so you just point at a random item and hope for the best. That's a bit like designing a user interface without understanding user motivation and behavior. Sure, it might look good, but it's not going to be very useful for anyone who wants to use it. So, how do we avoid this scenario and make sure we understand what our users want and how they behave?

The first step is to understand user motivation. Why are users coming to our website or app in the first place? What are they trying to achieve? Understanding their motivations will help us create designs that cater to their needs and goals. For example, if users are coming to a shopping website to buy a new pair of shoes, we need to make sure the shopping experience is easy and enjoyable. If users are coming to a news website, they might want to quickly scan headlines and read articles of interest. Understanding their motivations will help us create designs that are tailored to their needs.

The next step is to understand user behavior. How do users interact with our designs? What are their habits and patterns of behavior? Understanding user behavior will help us create designs that are intuitive and user-friendly. For example, if users are used to scrolling through content, we should make sure our designs are optimized for scrolling. If users are used to clicking on links, we should make sure our links are easily clickable. Understanding user behavior will help us create designs that are more usable and accessible.

Now, let's talk about the fun stuff. How can we make our designs enjoyable for our users? The answer is simple: add a bit of personality. No, we're not talking about hiring a clown to perform at your website launch party (although that could be fun). We're talking about adding a bit of personality to our designs. This could be as simple as using a unique color palette or font, or as complex as adding animations and micro interactions. Adding personality to our designs will make them more memorable and enjoyable for our users.

UI design is a lot like playing with Legos, only the blocks are made of pixels and the finished product is an app or website that people can interact with. Interaction psychology, on the other hand, is like a secret ingredient that makes the Legos even more fun to play with.

Think about it, if you're playing with Legos and they're just boring blocks that don't fit together, you're not going to have much fun. But when they're made to fit together in a certain way, they can be incredibly satisfying to build and play with. The same goes for UI design and interaction psychology.

Simplicity is also important in UI design. People don't want to be overwhelmed by too many buttons or confusing navigation. Designing interactions that are easy to use and understand is key to creating a positive user experience.

Feedback is also a crucial part of UI design. People need to know what's happening with the technology they're using. Designing interactions that provide clear feedback is essential to making sure users feel in control.

Confirmation is also important in UI design. People want to know that what they're doing is actually working. Designing interactions that provide confirmation can help to avoid frustration and improve the overall experience.

Mobile and desktop interactions are also different, so it's important to understand those differences. Mobile devices have smaller screens and are often used on the go, so designing interactions that work well on mobile devices is crucial.

Gamification is another important aspect of UI design. By making technology fun and interactive, you can encourage user engagement and improve the overall experience.

In conclusion, interaction psychology in UI design is like Legos and secret ingredients. By understanding the user-centered design process, the factors that affect user motivation and behavior, and the importance of simplicity, feedback, and engagement, you can design interactions that are both fun and effective. So go forth and play with your pixels, and make sure to add that secret ingredient of interaction psychology for maximum enjoyment.

13

---·---

APPLYING EMOTION IN UX/UI DESIGN

Simplicity in art is like a one liner joke, it's short, sweet and to the point, leaving a lasting impression without needing to overthink.

L et me tell you about the secret sauce that makes any boring tech project sizzle with excitement: Emotion! That's right, folks, we're talking about incorporating some good old-fashioned feelings into your UX/UI design projects. Why, you ask? Well, my friend, because it's the cherry on top of the sundae that is a user-centered product and experience. That's right, it's the icing on the cake, the sprinkles on the donut, the hot sauce on the tacos. You get the point.

Now, I know you might be thinking, "But wait, I thought this was a technical project, what does emotion have to do with it?" Well, that's the beauty of it all! Emotion plays a role that's bigger than a superhero's cape in how users perceive and interact with your products. It's like magic, but without the need for a wand.

So, how do we get this emotion in there, you ask? Easy peasy, lemon squeezy. Designers have an arsenal of strategies at their disposal to evoke specific emotions and create a positive user experience that's so good, users will be doing a happy dance. It's like a magician pulling a rabbit out of a hat, except in this case, its making users feel emotions so strong, they'll forget about their troubles for a moment.

As a UX/UI designer, one of the most important things you can do to make your product or service emotionally appealing is to get inside the head of your users. You need to know what makes them tick, what gets their hearts racing, and what makes them want to throw their computers out the window.

And how do you do this, you ask? Well, buckle up, pal, because we're about to embark on a wild ride through the world of user research and testing. It's like a treasure hunt for emotions!

First, you'll want to send out some surveys to get a general feel for what your users are feeling about your product. But don't stop there - you need to get up close and personal, so you'll also want to conduct some interviews and usability testing. This is where you'll really get to see how users respond to your product on a deeper, more emotional level.

Once you've got all that juicy data, it's time to get to work. You'll want to identify the emotional triggers and pain points that your users are experiencing, and then design solutions to help alleviate those feelings. It's like being a superhero, but instead of saving the world from evil, you're saving users from frustration and confusion.

Who says design can't be a wild and emotional ride? As UX/UI designers, we have the power to evoke all sorts of feelings in our users through the magic of color, typography, and imagery! Let's start with color - we can turn up the heat with bold reds and sizzling oranges, creating an environment of excitement and energy that'll make users want to jump out of their seats! Or maybe they want to chill out? No problem, just switch to cool blues and tranquil greens, creating a soothing atmosphere that'll have users feeling calm and relaxed in no time.

Now let's talk typography - want to add some extra oomph to your design? Use bold and expressive fonts that scream excitement and energy! But if you want to keep things relaxed, clean and simple typography is your best bet. By using these emotional design elements, you can create a UX/UI experience that truly resonates with your users, tugging at their heartstrings and leaving them with a lasting impression.

Designers have the power to tickle our emotions with their storytelling magic! That's right, folks, we use the art of storytelling to forge a bond between us and the products we design. Think of it as a fairy tale, but with a modern twist. We cast characters to represent the product, create an enchanted setting, and spin a captivating plot that helps us understand the product's purpose and value. It's like a magic spell that creates a sense of empathy and allows us to relate to the product on a deeper level.

Moving ahead, it's all about giving them the power! Yes, that's right, give them the reigns and watch their moods transform. No longer will they be stuck in the misery of frustration and anxiety, because they're in control! How do we do this you ask? Simple! We provide crystal clear directions, as if we're talking to a five-year-old (no offense to five-year-olds). And, if that's not enough, we let them customize and personalize their experience, like a bespoke suit tailor-made just for them. It's like we're saying, "Hey, you're the boss here. Do it your way, the right way."

Feedback is also the key to adding a little sass and flair to your UX/UI design. Picture this, you're using a product and suddenly, a little progress bar pops up and tells you, "You got this! You're almost there!" It's like having a personal cheerleader cheering you on through every step of the way. But wait, it gets even better! What if your actions were met with a satisfying "ding" or a cheerful "Yay, you did it!"? It's like having a virtual party every time you interact with the product. So, whether you want to go visual with progress bars and confirmation messages or auditory with sound effects and spoken feedback, just remember, feedback is the secret sauce that'll make your users feel like champions.

Now my fellow UX/UI designers, you can't just throw a little bit of emotion into your design and call it a day! Nope, it's a never-ending journey of reviewing, updating and getting feedback from those precious users. And let's not forget, we need to consider the big picture, the cultural and demographic context of our users. Because let's face it, not everyone reacts the same way to design elements, some may laugh, some may cry, and others may just give you a blank stare. So don't be afraid to put on your cultural anthropologist hat and get to know your users!

Remember, it's not just about making it pretty, it's about making it feel pretty! So, let's recap!

First, you gotta get inside their head. You need to know what they're feeling and why they're feeling it. So, you'll want to do some research and testing. It's like trying to figure out what someone's favorite color is, but for feelings!

Next, you want to add some emotional design elements. This could be anything from color to typography to imagery. Think of it like a painting. You want to use the right colors to evoke the right emotions.

But wait, there's more! You also want to tell a story. People love a good story, and they'll love it even more if they feel a part of it. So, sprinkle in some narrative elements and make sure your users feel like they're on a journey.

Now, you want to give them a sense of control and autonomy. This is like giving someone the keys to a car. They feel powerful and in control, and they love it!

And finally, don't forget to give feedback. This is like a pat on the back. It makes people feel good and lets them know they're doing a good job.

Now, let's dive into some case studies, shall we? We'll take a closer look at how emotional design has made a big impact on user engagement, satisfaction, and perception of a product. Think of it as a love letter from the digital world to its users. Get ready to laugh, cry, and maybe even fall in love with emotional design!

Picture this: You're cruising down the highway, belting out your favorite tunes, when suddenly your car transforms into a funky spaceship with laser beams blasting out of the speakers! That's the kind of experience you get when you step into the world of Spotify. It's like a funky carnival ride for your ears! With its bold typography, that's like a fist pump of excitement, and its slick color scheme, that's a mix of cool grays and bright accents, Spotify creates an atmosphere of pure musical bliss.

Spotify knows you like to be in control, so they've got you covered. They offer personalized playlists, like a BFF who knows your taste in music, and recommended songs, like a wise mentor who knows what you need before you do. It's like having a virtual DJ who's always got your back. And let's not forget the storytelling aspect. Spotify adds a touch of magic to your music, turning each song into a journey, making your playlist feel like an epic adventure.

Spotify is the epitome of emotional design, where visuals, personalization, and storytelling come together to create an unforgettable experience. It's like a musical roller coaster ride, where the music never stops and the excitement never fades.

Now, the Airbnb. The website that makes us all want to pack our bags and run away to a beachside villa, or maybe a cozy cabin in the mountains. It's a magical place where we can escape the mundane and live like royalty... for a few days at least. But have you ever stopped to think about why Airbnb has you feeling all warm and fuzzy inside? Well, my friends, it's all thanks to the clever folks at Airbnb and their mastery of emotional design in digital interfaces.

It's like they took a big pot of warm, comforting colors and slathered it all over the website. It's like a big, warm hug from a dear friend. And, if that wasn't enough, they went ahead and added a touch of storytelling and personalization, because why settle for just a warm hug when you can have a warm hug and a cup of tea, right?

You see, they feature pictures and reviews of the hosts and the properties, which is like getting a sneak peek into the life of the person you might be staying with. It's like a matchmaker's attempt to set you up with your ideal vacation rental. Will you be staying with a quirky artist who has a collection of vintage typewriters, or a grand-motherly type who bakes cookies for all her guests? You never know! And that's what makes it so darn exciting.

So, the next time you're scrolling through Airbnb, feeling all warm and fuzzy inside, remember it's not just the warm colors and cozy pictures, it's the magic of emotion-al design in digital interfaces. And if you're anything like me, you'll be booking your next getaway in no time!

Imagine this, folks, the masterminds behind Netflix have created a digital interface that will make your binge-watching experience so much more enjoyable. Say goodbye to boring and generic websites, and hello to the world of Netflix! With its bold typography and sleek black and red color scheme, you'll feel like you've entered a world of excitement and energy. It's like walking into a high-end club with a VIP pass, except you don't have to put on fancy clothes or deal with the long lines.

But that's not all, my friends. Netflix has taken it up a notch with its personalized features. Custom playlists and recommended shows are like having your own personal concierge, guiding you through the vast selection of content. It's like having a close friend who knows exactly what you want to watch, without you even having to ask.

And if that's not enough to convince you, Netflix also has a little something called storytelling. The website features trailers of the shows and reviews from real people, which helps you feel connected to the content and the experience. It's like having a sneak peek into the world of each show, without having to commit to an entire season. So, whether you're a drama junkie, a comedy aficionado, or a sci-fi geek, Netflix has got you covered.

Time for the wild and wacky world of Amazon! This website is a true master of emotional design, and let me tell you, it's no mean feat to make a website about shopping seem like a warm hug from your favorite aunt. But Amazon does it, oh yes, they do!

First off, they've got a clean and simple interface that's easy on the eyes, with a color scheme that's primarily yellow and gray, like a cloudy day with a silver lining. This creates a sense of trust and reliability that makes you feel like you're in good hands when you're browsing their wares.

But that's not all, no sir! Amazon also uses personalized features like custom recommendations and wishlists to make you feel like the website was made just for you. It's like they know you better than you know yourself! It's like they've been peeking over your shoulder at your browsing history and creating a shopping experience just for you. And you know what? It works! It keeps you engaged and motivated to keep shopping, because let's face it, who doesn't love feeling special?

And finally, we've got the cherry on top of this emotional sundae: feedback! Amazon features the reviews and ratings of the products, so you can see what other people think about what you're thinking about buying. It's like having a million shopping buddies who've already tried everything and are giving you the lowdown. And with all those opinions, you can make an informed decision and trust the products you're buying.

The secret to designing a digital interface that'll have users jumping for joy is all about getting in touch with their emotions. The likes of Calm, Netflix, and Amazon have got it all figured out. They've got their finger on the pulse of what users really want, and they're using all the tricks of the trade to keep 'em coming back for more.

Picture this: you're snuggled up on the couch, scrolling through Netflix and BAM! You come across a show that speaks to your soul. It's got just the right amount of personalization, with recommendations based on your viewing history. It's got storytelling on lock, with characters that you can't help but root for. And let's not forget the visual design elements - they're so on point, you feel like you're actually in the show.

But here's the thing, it's not a one-time deal. Emotional design is a never-ending journey. Think of it as a love affair with your users. You've got to keep the spark alive, keep up with the changing times, and listen to what they want. That's why it's important to continuously review and update your design based on user feedback.

And let's not forget, what may work for one person may not work for another. It's all about considering the cultural and demographic context of your users. Different cultures, different backgrounds, different emotional responses. So, if you want to design a digital interface that'll have users feeling the love, remember to keep it emotional, keep it personal, and keep it fresh.

Now, you might be asking yourself, "How do we even understand emotions in the first place?" Well, there are multiple methods and they're all different! We've got qualitative techniques like interviews and focus groups, and quantitative methods like surveys and experiments. It's like a choose your own adventure book, but with emotions.

But, without a doubt, the most popular and fun method is user interviews. This is where we get to ask users open-ended questions about their emotional experiences. It's like being a detective, but instead of solving a crime, you're solving emotions. How cool is that? This type of research is like gold, because it helps us understand the intricacies of emotions and what makes them tick. And the best part, we get to use this information to design products and experiences that tug at people's heartstrings. Who wouldn't want to be the mastermind behind that?

Okay folks, the focus groups! This is where a bunch of everyday people gather together to share their innermost feelings and emotional turmoil about a certain product or experience. And let me tell you, it's a wild ride! You never know what someone is going to say next, or how they're going to react to a certain product. It's like a roller coaster of emotions, with a whole bunch of laughs thrown in for good measure. But don't be fooled by all the giggles and guffaws, this type of research is actually quite important. It helps us understand how emotions are shaped by social and cultural norms, and reveals common patterns and themes across a group of users.

Moving to next planet, we have the survey method. It's like a multiple-choice test, but instead of answering boring questions like "What is the capital of France?" you get to answer exciting questions like "How intense do you feel when you see a cute puppy?" It's like a party in your brain and the survey is just along for the ride.

Next up, we have experiments. This is where the real fun begins! You get to see how different design elements affect your emotions. Think of it as a game of "What makes you feel happy or sad?" The best part? You get to be the guinea pig!

These methods are like the Keystone Cops of emotions and design. They provide hilarious insights into the workings of our emotional experiences and can even help designers identify the best gags (design elements) to tickle our funny bones. So, sit back, relax and enjoy the comedy of emotions and design.

Overall, this is no ordinary field of study, no sir! It's a complex, multi-headed monster that draws from psychology, sociology, anthropology, and design! *gasp* Yes, you heard that right, folks. This is a four-headed beast we're dealing with here. But fear not, for researchers and designers have a secret weapon - a combination of qualitative and quantitative methods. With these tools in hand, they're able to get a real deep dive into the emotional experiences of users and come up with designs that evoke the exact emotions they're after.

Alright folks let's wrap up this discussion on emotions in UX/UI design with a bang! To put it in simple terms, understanding emotions is crucial for creating killer products and experiences that leave users feeling like they've just gone on a wild ride with their emotions. By doing some user research and digging deep into the emotional experiences of users, designers can figure out the magic buttons to push in their designs. And let's be real, who doesn't love a good emotional rollercoaster ride?

But it's not just about making people feel things, it's about making sure those emotions are the right ones. The ultimate goal is to create designs that evoke the desired emotions and leave users with a smile on their face, a warm and fuzzy feeling in their heart, and a spring in their step. And let's not forget about the importance of considering social and cultural context. It's all about making sure everyone can enjoy the ride, regardless of who they are or where they come from.

As technology continues to evolve, so will the field of emotion-centered design. It's exciting to think about the possibilities of what designers will come up with in the future. We may be able to design experiences that make people feel like they're on a tropical vacation or that bring a tear to their eye. Who knows, the sky's the limit! So, let's all raise our virtual glasses and toast to the exciting future of emotion-centered design!

14

SHAPES IN DESIGN

Psychology of Shapes

*Gamifying your UI design is like adding sprinkles
to a cupcake - it's not necessary, but it sure makes
the experience sweeter and more enjoyable!*

L isten up folks, we've got a serious topic on our hands - shapes in UX/UI design! But don't worry, I'll make it fun, I promise. So, let's talk about shapes. Shapes, my friends, are the life of the design party. They're the DJ, the drink in your hand, and the hot dance moves all rolled into one. They're the foundational element that sets the mood for your interface. And let me tell you, they play a role as crucial as a superhero saving the day. They create an interface that's not only good-looking but also easy to navigate. In other words, they make your user's experience smooth as butter on a hot biscuit.

The world of UX/UI design! It's like trying to put together a jigsaw puzzle with a twist - you have to make sure all the shapes fit just right. And what's one of the key pieces to making this puzzle work? Visual hierarchies, my friend! It's like being a superhero and using your shapely powers to control the eyes of the user. With a wave of your magic wand (or mouse), you can make sure they're focused on the important stuff - like those big, juicy buttons that are screaming "CLICK ME, I'M IMPORTANT!" And for the not-so-exciting elements, well, you can use smaller, less flashy shapes to keep them in the background, like a supporting role in a Hollywood blockbuster.

Geometric shapes, such as squares and circles, can be a source of hilarious entertainment in the world of interfaces. These shapes are like the ringleaders of a circus, leading the user's eye to specific areas and creating a sense of order in the wild world of interfaces. It's like they are shouting, "Come one, come all! Look at this group of related elements!" while keeping everything else in line. They act as the bouncers of the interface, separating the different sections and making sure no one gets lost. It's like they are saying, "Sorry, you can't go there! That's for the other guys." But don't worry, with their simple yet effective ways, they'll have you laughing all the way through the interface.

Shape is like the magic wand of UX/UI design, adding a touch of wizardry to your interface. And one of the coolest tricks it can do is create an illusion of depth and dimension, making your interface look like a 3D movie. It's like when you watch a movie and you're like "How did they do that?" Well, shape does that with overlapping shapes that make your design look like it has depth and dimension. And if that's not enough, shapes can also create the illusion of movement by adding diagonal lines and gradients. So, your design will not only look 3D, but it will also feel like it's moving, making it a truly engaging experience.

Shapes also create visual cues that even a pirate with a peg leg could understand, like pointing arrows that say "Arrrrrrr, this way to navigation!" And they're also like a secret handshake, giving your brand a personality that's as unique as a parrot on your shoulder. Icons and logos become the cherry on top, like a pirate's flag, hoisted high for all to see.

Now, it's time for small recap! How shapes are important in the world of UX/UI design? It's like asking why carrots are important to Bug a Bunny. They're a crucial piece of the puzzle! Think about it, by carefully picking and choosing the size, color, and orientation of shapes, designers can guide your gaze like a GPS and make it super simple to navigate the interface. And let's not forget about the added benefits of shapes, like creating a sense of order, depth, dimension, and visual cues that will have users interacting with the interface like a pro. In short, shapes are the secret ingredient to making a user-friendly interface that's both intuitive and easy on the eyes!

Moving on, let's dive into the wild world of shapes and their impact on our brains. Shapes, my friends, are like the supermodels of the visual world, constantly affecting our perception and thinking in mysterious ways. Researchers have been trying to uncover the secrets of these shapely divas for years, peeking into the psychology, neuroscience, and cognitive science closets to get a glimpse of the truth. Get ready, because we're about to explore the many wacky ways in which shapes control our minds.

Our eyes are like shape-detecting ninja warriors, constantly on the lookout for the next big bad shape to conquer. Shape recognition is like a super power, and our visual system is like Professor X, helping us home in on those shapes faster than a speeding bullet! It's like we have X-ray vision for shapes, spotting them even in the craziest, noisiest of environments. This skill is vital for our survival, because let's face it, life can be full of danger and obstacles, and we need to be able to identify them ASAP! It's like we're always on high alert for shapely predators, ready to pounce at a moment's notice!

Shapes, my friends, are the masterminds behind our perception of space and layout. They're like the secret agents of our visual system, sneaking around to extract the positions and orientations of different shapes in an image so that we can navigate our surroundings with ease. This is crucial, especially when we're trying to manipulate objects or navigate through a new environment. Think of it as a game of Tetris - you gotta know the size and shape of those blocks to fit 'em all in, right? So, in essence, our ability to understand the layout of a scene and navigate through it is all thanks to the sneaky work of shapes.

Shapes have a way of sneaking into our noggins and taking control of our attention, like a bossy boss bossing around their minions. You know, like a boss. But seriously, scientists have discovered that our eyeballs are super smart and can pick and choose which shapes they wanna focus on based on their size, color, and any other fancy features they may have. It's like our eyes have a VIP list and shapes that meet the criteria get the royal treatment. But the fun doesn't stop there! Shapes also have a tight-knit relationship with our memory, like two peas in a pod. Our ability to remember shapes is all tied up with our ability to recall other visual details, like objects and scenes. It's like a game of "I Spy" with our memories.

Shapes also have the power to shape our emotions, research has uncovered that some shapes have the ability to stir up specific emotions like a witch's brew. For example, if you see a shape that's rounded and cuddly, it'll make you feel all warm and fuzzy inside, like a hug from your grandma. But, if you see shapes that are sharp and jagged, it'll make you feel all prickly and uneasy, like sitting on a cactus. It's like shapes are the emotional puppeteers, pulling our strings without us even realizing it! This emotional response is a big deal in fields like design, advertising, and art, so it's important to keep this in mind when you're creating something beautiful.

Well folks, you heard it here first - shapes are the new hot topic in the world of perception and cognition research! It's a wild, wild world out there in the shape-investigating biz, and the results are coming in faster than a toddler with a sugar high. You won't believe the latest findings - turns out our eyes can pick up on shapes like a boss and even extract fancy-schmancy concepts like symmetry, balance, and proportion! That's right, our brain is a genius when it comes to shapes, and it's all tied up with our love of pretty things. But wait, there's more! Shapes can also be influenced by all sorts of things, like our past experiences, culture, and even the weather (probably).

You see, experts in psychology, neuroscience, and design (like me) have spent countless hours studying this weird and wonderful phenomenon. They've uncovered all sorts of mind-boggling ways that shapes can influence our emotions and behavior, and they've even figured out the secret sauce behind it all.

The answer to the big question of "How do shapes affect our emotions?" is simple. It's all about the "affordances." That's just a fancy word for the natural traits of an object or shape that give us clues on how to play with it. For instance, imagine you're holding a round ball in your hand. Your brain automatically says, "Hey, this is a plaything, let's throw it around!" On the other hand, if you're holding a knife, your brain is like "Whoa, be careful! This is a weapon, not a toy!" This relationship between shapes and actions can evoke strong emotional responses, like feeling all warm and fuzzy when you see a round shape, or feeling a little uneasy when you see something sharp and jagged.

Shapes have some major emotional mojo going on, folks! It's all thanks to this thing called "archetypal associations." Basically, it means that certain shapes have a symbolic meaning that's been ingrained in our minds since the dawn of time. Take circles, for example. They're the shape of unity, completeness, and, like, never-ending awesomeness. On the flip side, triangles are the epitome of stability and brawn. So, when you see a circle, you'll probably feel all Zen and relaxed, but if you see a triangle, you'll feel like you could conquer the world. It's like a visual pep talk!

In the wild world of branding and marketing, companies are like magicians trying to evoke specific emotions with their logo's shapes and symbols. Take for instance, an eco-friendly company. They want their target audience to feel like they're saving the world one product at a time. So, they use a leaf or other natural symbol that makes you feel like you're hugging a tree and saving the planet, all at the same time. It's like a logo that gives you a warm and fuzzy feeling inside, without actually having to be warm and fuzzy.

You know what they say, "it's all in the shapes!" And boy, do shapes have a way of messing with our emotions and behavior. It's like they're sending secret signals to our brains, telling us how to act. For instance, have you ever noticed how you feel like taking a nap when you're surrounded by round shapes? It's not just a coincidence. Science has proven that round shapes, like a cozy couch or a round coffee table, make us feel relaxed and at ease. But on the flip side, if you find yourself in a room with sharp angles and jagged lines, you'll probably feel like you're stuck in a cage with a hungry lion. Yeah, angular shapes have a way of cranking up the tension and making us feel aggressive.

Shapes, my friends, are the building blocks of design greatness! They're the secret sauce that makes your branding sizzle and your user experience (UX) pop like a firecracker on the 4th of July. Without shapes, we'd all be wandering aimlessly through digital landscapes like lost sheep. But with shapes, we have the power to tell a story, evoke emotions, and create a visual identity that leaves an impression like a tattoo. Whether you prefer a simple circle, a complex geometric pattern, or a stylized version of a real-world object, shapes are the superheroes of UX/UI design, saving the day one pixel at a time.

Shapes are the foundation of all things branding. And let's be real, the most important shape of all is the logo. You know that little picture that's supposed to represent an entire company or product? Yup, that one. Logos are the epitome of first impressions, and they're the visual equivalent of a handshake (but with way more pixels). The shape of a logo can tell you everything you need to know about a brand. For instance, a circular logo says, "Hey there, we're all in this together." On the other hand, a logo with lots of sharp angles says, "Step back, we mean business." So, choose your shapes wisely, because they can make or break your brand.

Now, can I get a drumroll please? (drumroll) Ta-da! The power of color in branding is like ready to save the day with its emotional and meaningful abilities. Just think about it, a blue circle logo is like your trustworthy bestie who always has your back, while a red triangle logo is like a wild party animal that never fails to bring excitement. Colors, my friends, are the secret sauce in the branding world and also in the UX world.

Imagine walking down the aisle at the grocery store and suddenly, a colorful, quirky shape on a box of cereal catches your eye. That, my friend, is the magic of shapes in packaging. Companies use them to stand out and create a unique identity that's as recognizable as a celebrity's face.

And it's not just in the grocery aisle. Shapes are also used in advertising to draw attention to products and services, like a beacon calling out to you from a crowded magazine page. They're like a secret code that says "Hey, look at me!"

And last but not least, shapes are playing a crucial role in website design. They help create a sense of organization and hierarchy, making it easier for you to find what you're looking for. It's like a map that shows you exactly where the treasure is hidden.

Shapes are not just a simple doodle in your notebook, they are a crucial element in the grand design of creating a positive user experience (UX). In UX/UI design, shapes are like the road signs of the internet, guiding users through the digital world with ease and grace. Think about it, a button shaped like a triangle is like a little sign post that says, "this way to the specific function or page", while a circle is like a detour to a related action. Shapes also add a touch of sophistication, helping to organize the interface like a well-structured traffic system.

Did you know that shapes have a secret talent? They're the ultimate party crashers, showing up uninvited to make your interface a blast! They bring the fun by creating a consistent and familiar experience. Picture this: a company, dressed in their finest shapes and patterns, strolls into their website's header and footer and BAM! Cohesive visual identity. It's like a never-ending dance party where everyone knows the moves! But wait, there's more. Mobile apps are the ultimate shape-loving gurus, using a consistent set of shapes and colors to make navigation a breeze.

Geometric shapes have been causing a stir in the design world for centuries, and their popularity just won't go away! These shapes have been used in everything from ancient Egyptian hieroglyphs to today's snazzy branding and user interface design. They're like the LEGO blocks of design, always ready to be molded and shaped into something new and exciting! And let's be real, who doesn't love a good triangle or rectangle? These shapes add some much-needed flair to any design, conveying meaning and making the overall user experience more enjoyable.

Now, let's talk about the crazy world of geometric shapes and their wild adventures in design. These shapes are like the superheroes of the design world, each with their own unique powers. Circles are like the speedy Flash, zipping through the design with energy and movement. Triangles are like the cunning Catwoman, always ready to add a little edge and interest. And squares, well, they're like Superman, always there to bring stability and order to the chaos. But what happens when these shapes team up and form a pattern? That's right, folks, we've got ourselves a full-blown super team! Overlapping circles create a whirlwind of activity, making you feel like you're stuck in a tornado of excitement. Interlocking squares, on the other hand, are like the calm before the storm, bringing a sense of peace to the design. It's like a comic book come to life, folks!

Geometric shapes are the secret sauce to spicing up illustrations and graphics, my friends! You see, these shapes are like a box of crayons - there's a shape for every mood and emotion. Take for instance, a circle and triangle. These two shapes, when combined, scream unity and balance. It's like a love story between two shapes. And if you want to add some excitement to your graphics, the spiral shape is the way to go! This shape will take your graphics on a wild ride and convey the feeling of movement and growth.

Did you know that these shapes can be used to organize your website or mobile app like a boss? Picture it: a big, beefy square represents the main navigation button, like the king of the castle. Meanwhile, tiny circles and triangles scurry about like court jesters, indicating sub-navigation buttons. It's a visual hierarchy that's so clear, even a caveman could understand it. And what's more, users can navigate with ease, like a hot knife through butter.

Geometric shapes and color are a match made in design heaven. It's like a bad joke, with shapes being the setup and color being the punchline. They come together to create a visual story that's sure to make your audience feel something. Take the blue triangle for instance, it's like a trusty friend who always has your back. And the red circle, well that's like the life of the party - full of energy and excitement. But when you mix and match shapes and colors, it's like a wild party where anything can happen. A design party, if you will. The possibilities are endless and the emotions they evoke are a never-ending thrill ride.

Oh boy, have you ever heard the old saying "two shapes are better than one"? Well, it's true! When it comes to design, think about it, when you add a funky geometric shape as a background for a photo, it's like adding a funky hat to your outfit. It adds depth and movement to the image, making it stand out from the crowd. And let's not forget about typography, oh how boring would it be without some geometric shapes as a background?! It adds a sense of hierarchy and organization, making sure everything stays in its place.

Alright designers, we're gonna dive into some serious shape talk. You ready? When I say "shape", what's the first thing that pops into your noggin? I bet it's those boring old geometric shapes we see everywhere, like squares, circles, rectangles, and so on. But do you ever stop and think, what the heck do these shapes mean? Well buckle up, because we're about to find out!

Squares and rectangles, oh how we love thee! These shapes are like the bread and butter of the geometry world. Everywhere we look, we are surrounded by their straight lines and sharp angles. It's like they're the go-to shape for all things sturdy and dependable. Our walls, furniture, books, monitors, mobile phones, and even cameras all boast their square and rectangular shapes. It's like they're sending a message to the world, "Hey, I'm here, I'm strong, and I'm not going anywhere!" It's no wonder that these shapes evoke feelings of confidence, authority, and a sense of security. It's like they're saying, "Don't worry, I've got this!" So, the next time you see a square or rectangle, remember, they're here to bring you discipline, strength, courage, reliability, and a sense of security.

Triangles are the life of the shape party! With their pointy bits and energetic lines, they just scream "MOVE!" They've got direction and pizzazz, always ready to guide our gaze towards the top or wherever they're pointing. But watch out, these shapes are more than just fun and games. They've got a reputation! An upright triangle is all about stability and balance. It's like a yoga instructor in shape form. But flip that bad boy upside down and suddenly it's like we're at the edge of a cliff, with the triangle ready to plummet to its doom. That's why we get all nervous and jittery. So, let's recap the triangle's mood board: excitement, danger, risk, balance, and stability. These shapes are like a rollercoaster of emotions!

Circles, Ovals, and Ellipses - the never-ending story! These shapes are the epitome of eternal love, just like a wedding ring that never fades. Circles represent the sun, the Earth, and all the other sparkly objects in the universe, while ellipses are the whole cosmos itself - talk about grandiosity! Circles evoke a sense of mystery and enchantment, like a magician pulling a rabbit out of a hat. And let's not forget the best part, they don't have any pointy angles, making them as soft and cuddly as a kitten. So if you're looking to add some magic and mystery to your life, go ahead and embrace these circular wonders.

Spirals, those funky little swirls that can be found in all sorts of places in nature, like the spiral of a shell or the curl of a flower petal. But what do they mean? Well, to some, they symbolize the circle of life and growth, like a plant reaching for the sky. In other cultures, spirals are a symbol of wisdom and knowledge, like a wise old owl with a big brain. But in modern times, they're all about creativity and new ideas, like a bright young thing with a wild imagination. And let's not forget the calming influence of spirals, like a lazy cat stretched out in a sunbeam. So there you have it, spirals: growth, creativity, calmness, and intelligence all rolled into one little swirl!

Mother Nature is the real Picasso of our world! Just look at the way she effortlessly creates leaves that look like little green umbrellas, flowers that bloom like fireworks, and trees that reach towards the sky like they're trying to high five the sun. And let's not forget about the animal kingdom, where each creature has its own unique flair, from the majestic elephant to the sassy zebra. These natural shapes have inspired artists and designers for centuries, and they continue to do so today. Now, if you're wondering why Mother Nature's creations have such a strong influence, it's because they have a special significance. Each plant and animal have its own meaning, and they often bring a sense of peace and harmony to our lives. For example, a rose is a symbol of love and passion, while a lion represents pride and courage. In a nutshell, natural shapes represent originality, organic balance, and refreshment.

Now, let me tell you about these abstract shapes that have taken the design world by storm. They're like little cartoon characters, but instead of representing a recognizable object, they symbolize abstract concepts and ideas. Now, don't get too confused, some of these shapes can be pretty tricky to figure out. They're all dressed up in fancy clothes, and only a handful of features give away what they're meant to be. But here's the catch - each shape can mean two different things at the same time. It's like a magic trick, but with art. And let's not forget about the uniqueness factor. You see, these abstract shapes are like snowflakes, no two are exactly alike. They're each special in their own way, like a little snowflake, but instead of falling from the sky, they fall into the minds of graphic designers. Finally, these abstract shapes are perfect for graphic design, especially logos and icons. It's like a secret code between the designer and the viewer. No words needed, just a quick glance and the message is conveyed in a snap. It's efficient and elaborate, a true work of art. So there you have it, the intricate world of abstract shapes, where a little squiggle can mean so much more.

Shapes are the life of the party in the design world. They're the funky dancers on the dance floor, shaking their stuff to bring the room to life. Shapes play a vital role in creating designs that get noticed, whether it's as a visual component or a way to group elements together. Designers must be a shape wizard, understanding the magic that shapes cast on our minds and how to use that to their advantage.

Designers work with little wonders called logos and icons. A logo is like a brand's voice, and it must speak the right message. The right shapes in a logo can express the brand's attitude without saying a word. For instance, if a financial company's logo has shapes that convey trust and balance, like a square or triangle, then that company is in the money.

User interfaces in digital products are like a shape playground, with buttons, icons, and layouts. Designers use forms to arrange the content and make it easy to read and copy. For example, grouping text blocks in a rectangle or square helps users quickly grasp the information. Designers can also arrange the material in shapes to guide the user's eye to the important information. Like putting the cherry on top of the sundae, the material's peak should be the most significant component and arranged in a triangle shape.

Typography is another place where shapes rule. Different fonts styles have different influences on visual perception. Circular shapes are more feminine and gentler, while straight lines and sharp angles are more formal and sometimes even violent. Designers must choose their font wisely, making sure the shapes match the context and presentation.

The human mind is like a box of chocolates, you never know what you're going to get. But, with a little help from psychology, designers can understand how our brains work and create logos and user interfaces that solve problems. Designers who understand the psychology of shapes can create logos that speak the right message and user interfaces that make sense.

In conclusion, shape is like the star quarterback of the design team. It's got all the moves, all the skills, and all the charm to make your user interface touchdown in the end zone. But, like any good quarterback, you gotta know when to use those moves. Overuse will result in a penalty and misinterpretation is like a false start - it can really mess up the play. So, designers, let's huddle up and make sure we're using shape like a pro. We want interfaces that are beautiful, user-friendly and will have users cheering in the stands. Go team UX!

15

— . —

PSYCHOLOGY OF SOUNDS

Complexity in interface design is like trying to solve a Rubik's cube with a chainsaw, it may seem like a good idea at first, but the outcome is usually a mess.

Sound is like the magician of user experience design - it can make or break the show! When sound is used with wizardry and skill, it's like having a private symphony playing just for you. It sets the mood, directs your focus, and gives you a round of applause for every interaction you make. Think of it as the musical score to your life movie, and who doesn't want an award-winning soundtrack?

Sound, my friends, is like the frosting on the cake of user experience design. It can take your product or service from a mere "meh" to a "Wow, I'm so glad I clicked on this!" And let me tell you, we all want to be in the "Wow, I'm so glad I clicked on this!" camp, don't we?

So, let's start by talking about atmosphere. This is like the mood lighting of user experience design. A relaxing, Zen-like soundtrack in a meditation app can transport you to a peaceful island in the Pacific, where the only sound you hear is the gentle lapping of the waves against the shore. On the other hand, an upbeat, energetic soundtrack in a racing game can make you feel like you're the driver of a Formula One car, revving the engine and ready to zoom down the track.

Next up, we have attention-guiding sound. Think of it as your personal sound GPS. A satisfying "click" sound when you press a button, letting you know you've successfully taken an action. A notification sound letting you know that you've got a new message or some other exciting event.

Now, we come to feedback. This is the sound equivalent of a pat on the back. A "ping" when you complete a task successfully, or an error sound when you can't do what you wanted to do. It helps you understand what's going on, without having to read a manual or anything like that.

Last but not least, we have brand identity. This is where sound can give your product or service a personality. Imagine your company's logo accompanied by a unique sound. It's like a secret handshake, letting people know that you are part of the same gang.

But like with all good things, it's important to use sound judiciously. Too much sound can be like trying to have a conversation in a rock concert. It's also important to keep accessibility in mind. Not everyone can hear well, or may be in a noisy environment, so make sure your sound is appropriate.

The psychology of sound in UX/UI design is no laughing matter... or is it? In all seriousness, sound plays a major role in how we interact with digital products and design-ers need to have a solid understanding of the psycholog-ical principles behind it.

First things first, let's talk about attention. Our brains can only process so much information at once, so it's crucial for designers to use sound wisely to grab users' attention. Think about it, a soft ding for a button press and a loud siren for an error - these sounds guide users through their experience.

Next up, meaning. Our brains love making connections between sounds and their meanings, so designers need to choose their sounds wisely. A cheerful jingle for a positive outcome and a sad whistle for a negative one - you get the idea. And don't forget, the same sound can have different meanings in different contexts. For example, a door clos-ing sound could mean privacy at home, but confinement in a prison.

Affordance is also a big player in the psychology of sound. Sounds can suggest how to use an object, like a door closing sound indicating a menu has been closed. Lastly, the emotional impact of sound should never be underestimated. Different sounds can evoke different emotions in listeners, like a calming sound for relaxation or an exciting sound for urgency.

Sound has the power to make you feel all the feels! Let me tell you, it's a wild ride.

First of all, we have the concept of association. Our brains are like little detectives, always making connections between sounds and meaning. So, when we hear a bird chirping, it's like a symphony of peace and tranquility. But, when we hear a car horn, it's like a symphony of annoyance and frustration! It's amazing, right? Well, that's just the tip of the iceberg. Designers can use sound to create specific emotions in us by using these associations!

Next, we have the concept of memory. Sound has the power to trigger memories like a time bomb! For example, when you hear a familiar song, it's like a blast from the past, evoking feelings of nostalgia and longing. But, when you hear a baby crying, it's like a blast of tenderness and care! And guess what? Designers can use sound to trigger specific memories and past experiences, making us feel all the feels!

Thirdly, we have the concept of expectation. Our brains are like little futurists, always predicting and anticipating what's going to happen. So, when you hear a door opening, it's like you're entering a new world of excitement and adventure! But, when you hear a clock ticking, it's like the clock is ticking away your time! It's like a scene straight out of a movie, folks! And drumroll please, designers can use sound to create desired expectations and evoke specific emotional responses!

Finally, we have the concept of soundscapes. A soundscape refers to the combination of sounds that make up an environment. For example, a soundscape of a forest is like a symphony of peace and tranquility. But a soundscape of a busy city is like a symphony of stress and agitation! Designers can use soundscapes to create desired emotional responses in us, folks! It's like a symphony of emotions!

You know that feeling when you're sitting on the beach and the sound of the waves makes you feel all relaxed? Well, that's because sound has a profound impact on our physical and emotional well-being.

The human body is like a sound-absorbing sponge. Our ears take in sound waves, process them, and send them to the brain for interpretation. But, beware! Too much noise can damage the delicate structures of our ears, causing hearing loss and other auditory problems. So, if you're a sound designer, make sure you don't blast those tunes too loud or too long.

Sound has the power to stimulate the nervous system, affecting our emotions and physical well-being. Think of it as an emotional rollercoaster - the sound of waves can calm you down, while a fast-paced beat can get you pumped up. Designers can use this to their advantage, creating environments that promote physical and emotional well-being.

But watch out! Sound can also mess with your sleep patterns. Prolonged noise can disrupt your slumber, leaving you feeling tired and grumpy. But, on the flip side, exposure to calming sounds can promote relaxation and help you get a good night's sleep. So, if you're designing a sleep environment, like a hotel app or meditation app, make sure the sounds promote rest and relaxation.

And it's not just your sleep that's at risk - sound can also affect your cognitive function. Background noise can make it harder for you to concentrate and pay attention, but exposure to certain sounds, like nature sounds, can actually boost your cognitive function and promote relaxation. So, if you're designing a app for work or study environment, make sure the sounds help users focus and concentrate.

Last but not least, sound has a direct impact on our emotional well-being. Different sounds can evoke different emotional responses, and exposure to certain sounds can promote emotional well-being. Nature sounds can bring feelings of peace and tranquility, while music can bring joy and happiness. Designers must keep this in mind and use sound to promote emotional well-being in users.

Let's talk about the wild world of sound and its effects on our brainy bits. We've all heard of the Mozart Effect, where listening to classical tunes by the man himself can temporarily improve our cognitive abilities, specifically in spatial-temporal reasoning. But it's not just Mozart that can make us smarter, sound can also have an impact on our memory and perception.

Imagine a world where you're trying to work, but your coworkers are chatting up a storm. The background noise can mess with your cognitive performance, making you feel like you're in a war zone instead of an office. But fear not, there's a solution! Nature sounds and white noise can actually have a positive impact on your attention and performance. Now you can pretend you're in a serene forest while you crunch those numbers.

Sound can also influence how we perceive visual information. If you hear a sound that goes with a visual stimulus, you'll react faster than if the sound was out of place. It's like when you hear the satisfying "ding" of a notification and your eyes immediately go to your phone.

But hold your horses, these effects of sound on cognitive processes can vary from person to person and depend on the context. So, what's the solution? Incorporate sound in a user interface design, but do it carefully! Sound should add value to the user experience, not distract or confuse. Keep the sound design consistent, give users control over it, and test it to make sure it's effective.

Now, let's talk about different types of interfaces and their sound design. Mobile games love sound effects to enhance the gameplay, while financial apps use sound sparingly to avoid overwhelming users. E-commerce apps can use sound to create excitement, like when a customer makes a purchase. And let's not forget social media, where sound can indicate when a new message has been received or when a live video is about to start.

But hold on, let's not get too carried away just yet. While sound can be a powerful tool in creating a delightful user experience, it can also drive us absolutely bonkers if not used properly. That's why we've got to do some testing and evaluating to make sure we get it just right. And what better way to do that than with user testing?

User testing is like the Simon Cowell of sound design. It's going to give us some brutal honesty on whether our sound design is a hit or a miss. It can help us identify any issues, such as sounds that are too loud or confusing, and also help us determine if our sound is effective in enhancing the user experience.

So, let's get started with some testing methods! We've got A/B testing, usability testing, and surveys, oh my! A/B testing is like a sound design showdown. We'll pit two different sound designs against each other to see which one comes out on top. Usability testing is like a sound design spy mission. We'll observe users interacting with a user interface that includes sound to see how they react. And surveys? Well, surveys are like a sound design popularity contest. We'll ask users for their feedback on their experience with sound in a user interface.

Now, let's talk about some real-life examples of sound in UX/UI design. First, we have the use of sound cues in mobile apps. Mobile apps often rely on visual cues, but let's face it, sometimes we're too busy staring at our screens to even notice them. That's where sound cues come in, they're like a little tap on the shoulder to grab our attention. For example, the sound of a camera shutter letting us know we just took a fabulous photo, or a notification sound signaling a message has arrived.

Next, we have the use of ambient sound in virtual reality environments. Ambient sound is like a soundtrack for our virtual world. It can create a sense of immersion and realism, like the sound of birds chirping in a virtual forest or the sound of a train in a virtual train station. It can also signal changes in the environment, like when we move from one location to another, creating a sense of continuity and flow in the VR experience.

But, as with anything in life, there are also some not-so-successful examples of sound in UX/UI design. Let's talk about loud and distracting background music on websites or apps. Background music can be great for setting a mood, but if it's too loud or distracting, it can ruin the user's focus on the task at hand. Plus, background music that's not relevant to the website or app can cause confusion and frustration for the user. For example, heavy metal music on a retirement home website? Not a great idea.

Another example of unsuccessful sound in UX/UI design is the use of sound for notifications that aren't user configurable. Notifications are like little messengers, but if they're too loud or not configurable by the user, they can become a nuisance. For example, a website that plays a loud sound every time a new email arrives can be disruptive, especially if the user is in a public place or trying to work.

Sound is a crucial part of UX/UI design. It can enhance the user experience or detract from it. The key to success is to use sound judiciously and with the right psychological principles in mind. The principle of attention and context play a big role in the success of sound design.

In the end, sound is like a superhero in the world of user experience design. It can swoop in and save the day by providing helpful guidance, juicy feedback, and a sense of being fully immersed in the experience. But, like all good things, too much of it can be a real bummer. Overusing sound can make the user experience feel like a disaster movie. It's important to use sound with a light touch, so it can complement the visual design and support the user's mission. And let's not forget about our hearing-impaired friends. It's always important to consider accessibility and provide options for everyone to enjoy the superhero powers of sound. So, in short, sound can be a powerful tool for user experience designers to create an engaging and intuitive interface that will make users feel like they are in control.

16

PSYCHOLOGY OF COLORS

*Minimalism is like a tightrope walk between abun-
dance and emptiness. It's like a little rhyme with a
big impact.*

C olor, color everywhere and all the pixels look so
bright! Get ready for a wild ride through the world of
color psychology in UX/UI design, where hues and tints are
more than just pretty shades. It's time to learn how color can
influence emotions and behavior, and how to create engaging digital experiences with a splash of color!

First things first, let's talk about the role of color in UX/UI
design. It's like the glue that holds everything together. Col-
or creates visual hierarchy, directs the user's attention and
evokes certain emotions. Imagine a financial website or app,
and how you would feel if it was painted in bright pink. Not
exactly trustworthy, right? That's why blue is often used to

create a sense of security and trust. On the other hand, red is the color of urgency and excitement, making it perfect for calls to action or sale alerts.

Color perception is also affected by placement and contrast. Think of a red button on a white background. It stands out and grabs your attention like a clown at a funeral. But what if that same button was on a red background? It would blend in and be as noticeable as a squirrel in a forest.

Now, let's talk about branding. Color can be used to create a unique brand identity. For example, when you see the color green, you might think of money and banks. And who can forget the classic yellow of the sunshine-y fast food chain? By using a specific color palette, a brand can establish a strong visual connection with its audience.

But hold on to your paintbrushes, because color perception can vary greatly among cultures and individuals. White symbolizes purity and innocence in Western cultures, while in Eastern cultures it represents mourning and death. So, it's important to keep cultural differences and accessibility in mind when selecting colors for your design.

Let's start with the basics. You know that color wheel you see in art classrooms and museums? Well, it's basically a giant game of "Go Fish" for artists. The wheel is a visual representation of the love affair between colors. It's arranged in a circle with the primary colors (red, blue, and yellow) being the hotshots, secondary colors (orange, green, and purple) being the popular kids, and tertiary colors (red-orange, blue-green, etc.) being the awkward cousins.

Now, the color wheel is a tool to understand how colors interact and how to create color harmony. The simplest harmony is the complementary color scheme, where you use colors that are opposite each other on the wheel. For example, red and green are like peanut butter and jelly, blue and orange are like Batman and Robin, and yellow and purple are like...well, I don't know, maybe like sunshine and lavender. When you put these complementary colors together, it creates high contrast and makes your artwork pop.

Another popular color harmony is the analogous color scheme, which uses colors that are next to each other on the wheel. For example, red, red-orange, and orange are like a fiery sunset, blue, blue-green, and green are like a cool ocean wave, and so on. Analogous color schemes are like a big hug from your grandma, creating a sense of unity and flow.

Next up, we have the triadic color scheme, which uses colors that are evenly spaced around the wheel, forming a triangle. For example, red, yellow, and blue are like the American flag, and this harmony creates a sense of balance and variety.

And finally, the monochromatic color scheme, which uses variations of a single color. For example, using different shades of blue or different tints of yellow. This scheme is like wearing the same color outfit every day, creating a sense of harmony and unity.

But wait, there's more! There's also the split-complementary scheme, which uses a color and the two colors adjacent to its complement, and the square scheme, which uses four colors evenly spaced around the wheel.

Last but not least, it's important to remember that colors have psychological effects. Warm colors like red and orange can create a sense of excitement and energy, while cool colors like blue and green can create a sense of calm and tranquility. And let's not forget that colors can create different moods, like using yellow to create a sense of happiness or using black to create a sense of mystery.

Color is the MVP of visual hierarchy. It's the secret ingredient that takes your design from bland to beautiful. By carefully selecting and arranging colors, you can turn a bland page into a work of art that attracts the user's attention like a moth to a flame.

First up, let's talk color schemes. This is when you pick a set of colors that work together like peanut butter and jelly. These colors create contrast and draw attention to certain elements. For instance, if you want your call-to-action button to stand out, make it bright like a neon sign. And if you want your text to be easy on the eyes, make it darker than a moonless night.

Next up, contrast. This is when two colors are different in lightness or saturation. High-contrast colors stand out more and grab attention like a kid on a sugar high. So, if you want your important information to be seen, use bright red like a fire engine.

Now, let's add some depth to our design with color gradients. This is when one color gradually blends into another. It creates an illusion of depth and makes your design look like a 3D movie. For example, you can make a background image appear more dynamic with a gradient or make a button look like it's popping out of the screen.

Last but not least, let's talk color coding. This is when you use different colors to represent different types of information. For instance, use blue to represent links and red to represent errors. It makes it easy for users to quickly identify and understand different types of information on the page, just like a traffic light.

Coloe is one thing that can make your brand go from drab to fab in a jiffy! And, if you want to make sure your brand is the life of the party, you better make sure you get your color scheme right.

First of all, let's talk about why color is so important in branding. It's simple, my friends, color can evoke emotions, memories and create a strong visual association with your brand. Just think about Coca-Cola's iconic red color - it's synonymous with the brand and immediately recognizable. The same goes for Facebook's shade of blue. When people see that color, they immediately think of the social media giant.

Now, when it comes to choosing your brand's color scheme, you need to make sure it's appropriate for your industry and target audience. For example, a law firm might want to go for a more traditional and professional look with colors like navy blue and gray, while a children's toy company might want to go for a more playful look with bright colors like red and yellow.

Once you've got your color scheme sorted, it's important to make sure you're consistent with it. That means using the same colors across all your branding materials - your website, packaging, advertising and any other marketing materials. Consistency is key in creating a recognizable and memorable brand image that people will associate with your business.

And, while we're talking about consistency, let's talk about typography. The color of your text should be consistent across all your materials and easy to read. So, if you've got a dark blue color in your brand scheme, make sure your text is a lighter color like white or gray to ensure it's legible.

Finally, make sure you're using your brand's colors in the right context. For example, don't use a color that's associated with a negative emotion or connotation for a call-to-action button on your website. You want your brand's color to be consistent with your messaging and values.

The squiggly lines and shapes we see every day that makes life a little more exciting and less dull. And as designers and artists, it's our job to make sure we understand the ins and outs of these rainbow hues to create designs that are not just visually appealing but functional too!

Now, we need to know what the people want, and that's where user research comes in. You might think you know what colors people love, but you'll be surprised how much you don't! Surveys, interviews, focus groups, and usability testing, these are some of the methods we use to get a deeper understanding of how colors affect users' emotions and behavior. And with that information, we can create designs that are more user-friendly and visually appealing.

But where do we start with choosing colors? With so many tools and resources available, it can be a bit overwhelming. Fear not, my friends! With a little bit of knowledge and exploration, you'll be able to navigate these tools with ease. Adobe Color (formerly Adobe Kuler) is a popular online tool that lets you create, save, and share color palettes. Canva's Color Palette Generator is another great tool that generates a color palette based on an image you upload. And for physical color swatches, Pantone's color guides are a go-to for many designers.

And what about color theory? That's where color wheel tools come in. Adobe's Color Wheel is a great digital tool that allows you to experiment with different color combinations and harmonies. And if you're curious about the psychology and emotional impact of different colors, the Color Affects system is a great resource.

So, you've chosen your colors, but how do you make sure they look good in all contexts? Testing, testing, and more testing! Make sure you view your color palette in different lighting conditions and on different devices, as colors can appear differently on a computer screen compared to print.

Now, let's talk about color accessibility and contrast. These elements play a crucial role in making sure all users, including those with visual impairments, can understand and interact with your content. Understanding the different types of color blindness and how they affect color perception is key in creating accessible color schemes. You should avoid using colors that are too similar to each other and use high-contrast colors for text and other elements. The World Wide Web Consortium (W3C) has established guidelines for contrast ratios, and using color contrast tools can help you make sure your designs meet these guidelines.

And last but not least, don't forget to provide alternative ways for users to access your content. Text descriptions for images and videos, captions for audio content, and other accessibility needs should always be considered.

Color management systems have taken the design world by storm and are basically the superheroes of the design world. They've made it possible for designers to have a "color-match guarantee" by letting them create, edit and display images with stunning accuracy. No more panicking about if the colors you see on your screen will match the final product, it's like having a trusty sidekick by your side.

Digital painting and illustration tools, like Adobe Photoshop and Corel Painter, have also caused quite the buzz. These tools have made it possible for artists to create digital paintings that are so realistic, it's like they were painted by Leonardo da Vinci himself. And the best part? Artists can now play around with color like never before, adjusting and customizing digital brushes to create a rainbow of effects.

The internet and mobile devices have also had a significant impact on digital design and color. With more and more people accessing the internet on their tiny screens, designers have to keep in mind the limitations of small screens and lower resolutions. So, they've focused on keeping designs simple and minimal, striking to the eye and easy to navigate on small screens.

Looking into the future, we can expect to see some major changes in digital design and color. OLED and QLED screens are the new kids on the block and they're here to stay. These screens offer brighter and more vibrant colors with higher contrast ratios, making the digital world even more magical.

Virtual and augmented reality is also making waves in the digital design world. These technologies allow designers to create immersive experiences that transport users to new worlds. As technology continues to improve, we can expect to see more and more designers exploring the possibilities of VR and AR in their work.

Finally, we have the big guns - machine learning and artificial intelligence. These technologies have the potential to change the game for designers by automating tedious tasks like color matching and image editing. This means designers can focus on more creative aspects of their work and let the machines do the heavy lifting. So, sit back, relax and let the future of digital design and color blow your mind!

In the end, color psychology in UX/UI design is like a secret sauce for designers. It's the key ingredient to making designs that are not just pretty to look at, but also effective in keeping users engaged and satisfied. By using colors that are fitting for the target audience and purpose, designers can create designs that are easy on the eyes and a breeze to navigate. Color psychology can also be used to build trust and credibility, and guide users through the design like a trusty tour guide. In short, designers should learn about color psychology and how it can be used in their designs. It's like adding sprinkles to an already delicious ice cream cone. You don't need it, but it sure makes the experience better! So, don't be afraid to experiment and have fun with color psychology, and create designs that are not only beautiful but also successful in achieving their intended goals.

17

— • —

Psychology of Typography

Building a website is like crafting a Ferrari, not cranking out Fords like a factory assembly line. It's all about quality, not just churning out numbers!

Ah, the glorious art of typography! It's like putting together a jigsaw puzzle, but instead of boring old pictures, you get to play with letters, numbers, and punctuation marks! Who wouldn't want to do that all day long?

So, let's go back to where it all began. Imagine a world without printers, without computers, and without any sort of mass-production of information. That's right, folks, we're talking about the Dark Ages, also known as the 15th century. Back then, if you wanted a copy of a book, you had to copy it by hand. That's like writing a novel with a feather and inkwell, every time you want to read it.

Enter our hero, Johannes Gutenberg, who decided enough was enough and invented the printing press. This changed the world forever and allowed us to produce books, newspapers, and other printed materials quickly and cheaply. And it all started with movable type, which was essentially a box of individual letters and symbols that could be arranged to form words and sentences. Genius, right?

And we've been improving ever since! The 16th and 18th centuries brought us new typefaces like Garamond and Baskerville, adding even more elegance and readability to printed materials. And then in the 19th century, lithography was invented, which allowed for even greater flexibility in design.

But the real game-changer came in the 20th century, when digital technology arrived on the scene. The first digital typeface was created in the 1970s, and since then, the sky has been the limit! Computers have made it possible to create and manipulate type in ways we never even dreamed of. Nowadays, typographers have access to an almost endless variety of typefaces and can create designs that are customized to specific audiences and purposes.

But let's not forget that typography isn't just about making text look good. It's also about making it easy to read and understand. Good typography guides the reader's eye through the text, making it more accessible and helping the information stick. It's an essential element of graphic design, web design, and even motion graphics.

Now, are you ready to get all sorts of type-faced? Because I'm about to dive into the wild world of font styles!

First up, we have the classic serif typefaces. These are the ones with little lines or frills on the ends of each letter's strokes. Times New Roman, Garamond, and Baskerville are all big players in the serif game. These types of fonts are perfect for traditional printed materials, like books and newspapers, because the little serifs make it easier for your eyes to travel down the page without getting lost.

Next, we have the sans-serif typefaces, which are characterized by their smooth, simple lines. Arial, Helvetica, and Futura are some of the most popular sans-serif fonts. These are the perfect fonts for digital mediums like websites and mobile apps, because they're easier to read on screens.

Now, let's take a stroll down script lane. Script typefaces are designed to look like handwriting or calligraphy, and they're often used for fancy events, greeting cards, and other formal documents. Brush Script, Lucida Handwriting, and Papyrus are a few of the many script typefaces out there.

And finally, we have the display typefaces. These are the fonts that love to be the center of attention, as they're designed for large text like headlines and titles. Impact, Rockwell, and Cooper Black are just a few of the many display typefaces available.

In addition to these four main types, there are also sub-categories and variations. For example, monospace type-faces have characters with the same width, while propor-tional typefaces have characters with different widths. And there are even typefaces specifically designed for certain languages, like Chinese or Arabic.

Now, choosing a typeface is like picking out an outfit for a fancy party - it's important to consider the occasion and audience. Serif typefaces might be more appropriate for a book, while sans-serif fonts might be better for a website. And don't forget about the overall design and aesthetic - the typeface can make a huge impact!

Typography is like a magic wand for making written mate-rials more readable and engaging. The typeface, font size, line spacing, and use of white space can all work together to create an easy and comfortable reading experience. For example, larger font sizes are generally more legible, but too much big text can become overwhelming. And don't forget about the power of white space - it can make or break the readability of your text.

But in all seriousness, typography is a crucial element in creating a website that's easy on the eyes and easy to use. It's like the makeup on a supermodel, it makes everything look better! And just like makeup, there are so many different aspects to consider when it comes to typography.

First up, let's talk legibility. This is all about making sure the text is crystal clear, so the reader doesn't have to squint their eyes to figure out what the heck they're looking at. This is achieved by using font sizes that are big enough to read, with enough space between the lines and the letters. Think of it like giving your readers a hug, you want them to feel comfortable and happy while they're reading.

Next up is readability. This is all about making sure the text is easy to understand. You don't want your readers to have to use a dictionary every time they visit your website. This is why it's important to have a consistent hierarchy of headings, subheadings and body text. And don't forget to break up the text into manageable chunks, so your readers don't get overwhelmed.

But typography isn't just about functionality, it's also about style. Different typefaces, font sizes and colors can be used to create a visual interest and guide the reader's attention to the most important content on the page. It's like putting together an outfit, each element contributes to the overall look and feel.

And speaking of look and feel, let's not forget about brand identity. The typeface, font size, spacing, alignment, and color of the typography can all be used to communicate a brand's message and create a sense of familiarity for the reader. It's like a secret handshake between the brand and the reader.

The typeface is like the hairstyle of the typography world, it sets the tone for the whole look. Different typefaces can convey different emotions and messages, like a serif typeface for a more traditional and formal brand, or a sans-serif typeface for a more modern and casual brand.

The font size is like the jewelry of the typography world, it can make a bold statement or be understated. The font size can be used to create a sense of hierarchy and importance, with larger font sizes for headlines and smaller font sizes for body copy.

The spacing and alignment are like the shoes of the typography world, they can convey balance and symmetry or movement and energy. A brand that wants to convey calm and stability may use evenly spaced and aligned typography, while a brand that wants to convey excitement and energy may use uneven spacing and alignment.

And finally, the color of the typography is like the nail polish of the typography world, it can add the finishing touch. Different colors can convey different moods and emotions, like red for passion or blue for trust. And the color of the typography can also be used to create contrast and hierarchy, with bold and bright colors for headlines and subdued colors for body copy.

Typography is the aspect of design that packs a punch, the one that can make or break a website or app's engagement and conversion rates.

Think of typography as a superhero, fighting the good fight against boring and unreadable text. Its secret weapon? A clear, legible font and font size that make it easy for users to understand the content on the page. And what's a superhero without a sidekick? Typographic hierarchy comes to the rescue, presenting different levels of text in different font sizes and styles to guide users through the content and make it more engaging.

But wait, there's more! Typography is also a master of disguise, using bold and attention-grabbing headlines to draw users in and encourage them to take action. And it's not just about grabbing attention, typography also knows how to get the job done by using clear and concise call-to-action phrases to increase conversion rates.

Contrast is also a crucial part of typography's arsenal. High contrast between text and background is like a beacon of light, making text legible and easy to read, while low contrast is like a dark, creepy alley that makes users run for the hills.

And what's a superhero without some spacing? Typography knows the importance of keeping things organized and legible, with adequate spacing between lines and characters. Too little spacing, and it's like a crowded and confusing market, causing users to quickly lose interest.

But it's not just about being practical and functional, typography also knows how to have a good time! It uses playful, whimsical fonts to create a lighthearted and fun atmosphere, while elegant, serif fonts convey sophistication and professionalism. These subtle design choices can greatly influence the overall user experience and can help establish the brand's identity.

The art of arranging letters on a page can be pretty darn funny. Who knew? But in all seriousness, typography is not just a boring old functional aspect of design, it's a powerful tool that can make or break your message.

Let's start with the font choice. It's like choosing a costume for your letters. Different fonts can evoke different emotions, just like different costumes can evoke different emotions in humans. For example, have you ever seen someone walk into a fancy party in a banana suit? The audience might perceive that person as silly and fun-loving. In the same way, a serif font like Times New Roman might evoke feelings of intelligence and authority, while a sans-serif font like Arial might evoke feelings of simplicity and functionality.

Now let's talk about spacing and arrangement. It's like giving your letters a dance partner. The way letters are spaced and arranged can greatly impact their legibility and readability, just like how having a good dance partner can impact your dancing. If the letters are too close, it might look like they're bumping into each other and make the text difficult to read. On the other hand, if they're too far apart, it might look like they're shy and not connected to each other. But if you find the right balance of spacing and arrangement, your letters will dance gracefully and make the text enjoyable to read.

Typography also has the power to influence our emotions. It's like adding some musical notes to your letters' dance. The use of certain elements such as bold, italic, and underlining can add emphasis and draw attention to certain words or phrases. This can help convey the intended emotional tone of the text. And don't forget about color! It's like adding some lights to the dance floor. Warm colors like red and yellow can evoke excitement and energy, while cool colors like blue and green can evoke calm and tranquility. By carefully selecting the right elements, a designer can create a desired emotional response in the reader, just like how a DJ can create a desired mood on the dance floor.

Typography also affects our memory and recall. It's like recording a video of your letters' dance. The way text is presented can impact how our brains process and retain information. Clear, legible fonts and appropriate font sizes can improve readability, just like how having a good camera can improve the video quality. Similarly, the use of typographic hierarchy can guide the reader and make the text more memorable, just like how having a good director can make a video more memorable. And don't forget, the use of attention-grabbing headlines and specific font styles and aesthetics can help establish a brand's identity and create a specific tone for the text, making it more memorable.

Now let's look down on some examples, first, let's take a look at Apple's website. It's known for its minimalist design aesthetic, but it's also known for its funny typography. The font used is a variation of the classic San Francisco font and it's designed specifically for digital screens. So, basically, it's a font that was made to be funny. And it is! The font size is large, making it easy to read on any device, and the use of white and negative space creates a sense of clarity and simplicity. The result? A website that's easy to navigate, easy to read, and will have you laughing out loud. Trust us, the website's so funny, even the most serious people can't help but crack a smile.

Next up, we have the website for the New York Times. Now, this one's a bit more sophisticated, but that doesn't mean it's not hilarious. The typography used on the website is elegant and sophisticated, with a focus on readability and legibility. The font used is a variation of the classic Times New

Roman font and it's designed specifically for digital screens. The font size is large, making it easy to read on any device, and the use of white and negative space creates a sense of clarity and simplicity. The result? A website that's both sophisticated and hilarious, and will leave you in stitches.

And let's not forget about the popular websites and apps like Facebook, Instagram, and Twitter. They all use typography effectively in their UX/UI design and they're all hilarious. Facebook uses a clean and simple typography, with a focus on legibility and readability. The font used is a variation of the classic Helvetica font, designed specifically for digital screens, and the font size is large, making it easy to read on any device. Instagram uses a playful and fun typography, with a focus on legibility and readability. The font used is a variation of the classic Futura font, designed specifically for digital screens, and the font size is large, making it easy to read on any device. And Twitter uses a clean and simple typography, with a focus on legibility and readability. The font used is a variation of the classic Arial font, designed specifically for digital screens, and the font size is large, making it easy to read on any device.

But not all examples of typography in UX/UI design are effective and hilarious. In real-world examples, typography can often be poorly executed, resulting in a confusing and frustrating user experience. Take the website of the State Bank of India, for example. The typography used on the website is cluttered and confusing, with a focus on style over legibility and readability. The font used is a script font, which is difficult to read on digital screens, and the font size is small, making it difficult to read on any device. The use of too many different font styles and sizes creates a sense of chaos and confusion. The result? A website that's so funny, it's not even funny.

At the end of the line, typography is like the conductor of an orchestra in UX/UI design. It makes sure all the information is in order and easy for users to follow, like a well-organized marching band. By picking the right musical notes (aka typefaces), adjusting the volume (font size), and creating harmony with spacing and contrast, designers can make sure the user experience is as smooth as a symphony. Typography can also be used to showcase a brand's unique identity, like a personal signature on a painting. To sum it up, taking typography seriously can make your digital product a hit and make sure users have a toe-tapping good time.

18

UI DESIGN-THE FINE ART OF MAKING SCREENS LOOK BEAUTIFUL

Time's a-ticking, so don't waste it being a boring clone of someone else's existence. Live life like it's golden, not like it's borrowed!

UI design, also known as user interface design, is like the make-up of a digital product. Think of it as a top-notch digital makeover that transforms a website or mobile application from drab to fab! It's all about making technology look and feel good, so that it's not just easy on the eyes, but also easy on the mind. And let's be real, in today's world where technology has become our BFF, a good UI design is more important than ever.

UI design isn't just about pretty colors and cute graphics. It's also about making sure things work like a well-oiled machine. The design should be user-friendly, easy to navigate, and super-efficient. It should be like a smooth ride in a sports car, where the design should make you feel like a pro even if you've never driven before. A UI designer is like a superhero, who has the power to understand the needs of the users and create a design that is not only stunning but also meets their needs.

UI design is a problem-solving process that requires a designer to have a deep understanding of the user's needs, the business goals, and the technical limitations. The designer must have the skills to put on their thinking cap and come up with a design that is not only pleasing to look at but also solves the problems at hand. It's like being a detective, where the designer must gather all the clues, analyze them, and come up with a solution that fits the bill.

Usability is the key to unlocking the full potential of UI design. A UI designer must understand how users interact with digital products and create a design that is so intuitive, even a 5-year-old could figure it out. And if the user does make a mistake, the design should have built-in error recovery solutions that make it a breeze to get back on track. It's like having a safety net in a circus act, where even if you slip, you can still bounce back.

Accessibility is also a crucial aspect of UI design. A UI designer must understand the needs of users with disabilities and create a design that is inclusive and accessible to all. This includes designing for users with visual, auditory, and motor impairments, and making sure that technology is accessible to everyone, regardless of their abilities. It's like building a bridge, where the designer must make sure that everyone, no matter their physical abilities, can cross it with ease.

UI design is always changing and evolving, like a chameleon. New technologies and trends are always popping up, and a good UI designer must be able to adapt and stay up to date. They must be able to think outside the box and come up with innovative solutions that push the boundaries of what is possible. It's like being a mad scientist, where the designer must always be experimenting and coming up with new and exciting ideas.

Types of User Interfaces

User Interface is the magic that allows us to interact with our digital devices and make them do our bidding. It's the bridge between our thoughts and the digital world. And like all good bridges, there are different types to choose from.

First up, we have the GUI, or Graphical User Interface. This is the most common type of UI and it's the one you probably use every day without even realizing it. It's like the wise old grandfather of UIs, the one you turn to when you need to get things done quickly and easily. GUI interfaces use graphical elements, like icons, buttons, and menus, to help you navigate and control the digital product.

Next, we have the VUI, or Voice User Interface. This is the new cool kid on the block. With the rise of smart speakers and virtual assistants, VUI interfaces are becoming more and more popular. These interfaces use voice commands and natural language processing to help you control your digital product. It's perfect for those moments when you want to keep your hands free, like while driving or cooking. It's also great for users who have trouble using a keyboard or mouse.

And finally, we have the Gesture-based interfaces. This type of UI is like the fun, adventurous cousin of the UI family. These interfaces use gestures like swipes, taps, and pinch-to-zoom to help you interact with your digital product. They're commonly used on touchscreen devices and are designed to be intuitive and easy to use. It's like you're dancing with your device!

Each type of UI has its own unique benefits and limitations, so choose wisely! GUI interfaces are easy to use, but can be less flexible. VUI interfaces are hands-free, but can be less accurate. Gesture-based interfaces are intuitive, but can be less precise. But hey, like they say, it's all in the wrist!

Designing for Humans Not Bots

UI design, you see, is all about making sure the user has a positive experience. It's about making sure they can complete their tasks with a smile on their face, without pulling their hair out in frustration. And let's be real, nobody wants a frustrated user.

So, what's the secret to a good UI design? Well, allow me to introduce you to the 10 principles of Dieter Rams. This legendary industrial designer knows what's up when it comes to UI design. Let me break it down for you:

1. **Innovative** - It's got to be fresh and new. Not your grandma's UI design.

2. **Useful** - It's got to serve a purpose. No nonsense, all functionalities.

3. **Aesthetic** - It's got to look good. Beauty is in the eye of the beholder, but UI design has got to be a feast for the eyes.

4. **Understandable** - It's got to be easy to understand. No rocket science, just simplicity.

5. **Unobtrusive** - It's got to blend in with the overall experience. No show-offs allowed.

6. **Honest** - It's got to be true to its purpose. No lies, no deception.

7. **Long-lasting** - It's got to be durable. Timeless quality is key.

8. **Thorough down to the last detail** - It's got to be well thought out and executed. No missed opportunities.

9. **Environmentally friendly** - It's got to consider the planet. Sustainability is a must.

10. **As little design as possible** - It's got to be minimalistic. Only what's necessary, nothing more.

By following these principles, UI designers can create interfaces that are intuitive, efficient, and enjoyable. It's not just about making screens look pretty, it's about creating an overall experience that the user will love.

UI design is a fine art indeed. It takes a combination of technical skills, artistic talent, and attention to detail to create interfaces that are not just functional, but also a pleasure to use. It's about understanding the user, providing them with a seamless experience, and making sure they keep coming back for more. In today's digital age, UI design is more important than ever. With so many devices and platforms, it's essential to have a UI design that can adapt to all screens and devices. UI designers must be able to stay ahead of the curve and create interfaces that are beautiful, responsive, and accessible.

In a nutshell, UI design is a wild ride that takes a whole lotta heart and smarts! It's like a delicious cake made with equal parts of technical know-how and artistic flair. It's about taking the dull screens of the world and turning them into eye candy with a side of ease-of-use. It's about giving users an experience that's so smooth and fun, they'll want to ride it again and again!

19

UX-CEPTIONAL: THE QUEST FOR STRATEGIZING INTERFACES THAT STAND OUT

We're on a mission to make a big ol' crack in the universe, 'cause if not, why bother showing up in the first place?

Gone are the days of clunky and confusing interfaces that left users feeling like they were lost in a labyrinth of buttons and menus. Today, UX Design is the shining star of digital design, where the focus is on making interfaces so user-friendly that even your grandma could use them (yes, even your grandma!).

UX Design is like a magician, taking the raw materials of psychology, design, and technology, and turning them into interfaces that are so intuitive, you'll forget you're even using them. The secret to the magic is in the process, understanding the user's needs, behaviors, and goals, and using that information to create interfaces that are easy to navigate, visually pleasing, and efficient.

In the early days of computing, interfaces were like reading a foreign language, with text-based commands that required a PhD in computer science to understand. But then came the graphical user interfaces (GUIs), and suddenly, even your grandma could use a computer.

With the rise of the internet and mobile devices, the demand for even more user-friendly interfaces skyrocketed. This led to the development of Human-Computer Interaction (HCI) and the User-Centered Design (UCD) process, putting the user at the center of the design process. And voila, the interfaces became so user-friendly that even your grandma's cat could use them!

Today, UX Design is a vital part of the digital design process, with a focus on creating interfaces that are not only functional but also intuitive and enjoyable to use. It's like putting on a comfortable pair of shoes, it just feels right. And as the field continues to evolve, new trends and technologies are emerging that are taking UX Design to new heights. Virtual and augmented reality, artificial intelligence, and the Internet of Things are just a few examples of these exciting technologies that are being integrated into interfaces to create truly immersive and personalized experiences.

So, what does the future hold for UX Design? It's a never-ending quest for the perfect balance of function and form, usability and aesthetics, and technology and human behavior. But through this quest, the field of UX Design continues to evolve and improve, leading to interfaces that are not only functional but also truly exceptional. It's a journey worth taking, and we can't wait to see where it leads us next!

Principles for the Inner Peace of Your Users

As UX Designers, we're basically professional problem-solvers and life-simplifiers for our users. But how do we go about doing that?

First up, we have User-centricity. This is like the dating advice of UX Design. It's all about putting yourself in the user's shoes and thinking about their needs, behaviors, and goals. We gather intel by conducting research, gathering data, and conducting user testing. This way, we can create interfaces that are specifically tailored to their needs, making their experience a smooth and enjoyable one.

Next, we have Consistency. This is like the wardrobe advice of UX Design. It's all about creating a sense of familiarity and predictability for the user. Consistency means using similar design elements throughout the interface, like using the same font and color scheme. It also means using similar language and labeling conventions, making it easy for the user to understand and navigate the interface. Consistency helps build a sense of trust and confidence in the user, making them feel comfortable and in control.

Third on the list is Hierarchy. This is like the traffic advice of UX Design. It's all about creating a logical order and structure for the interface. It means organizing information in a way that is easy to understand and navigate. Hierarchy helps guide the user's attention to the most important information and actions, making it easy for them to complete their tasks.

Next, we have Context. This is like the weather advice of UX Design. It's all about understanding the user's environment and the tasks they are trying to complete. It means taking into account the user's location, device, and other factors that may affect their experience. By understanding the user's context, we can create interfaces that are tailored to their specific needs and make their experience more seamless and efficient.

Fifth on the list is User Control. This is like the personal finance advice of UX Design. It's all about giving the user control over their experience. It means providing the user with options and allowing them to make choices. User control helps create a sense of ownership and empowerment in the user, making them feel more in control and satisfied with their experience.

Sixth, we have Accessibility. This is like the equal rights advice of UX Design. It's all about making sure the interface can be used by everyone, regardless of their abilities. It means creating interfaces that are accessible to users with disabilities, like those who are visually impaired or have mobility issues. Accessibility helps create an inclusive and equitable experience for all users.

Last but not least, we have Usability. This is like the cooking advice of UX Design. It's all about making sure the interface is easy to use. It means creating interfaces that are simple, intuitive, and efficient. Usability helps ensure that the user can complete their tasks quickly and easily, making their experience more enjoyable and satisfying.

And remember, always add a pinch of humor to your design process. It not only makes the work more fun, but it also helps create a more memorable experience for the users.

In conclusion, we've learned about the key principles of UX Design, like putting the user first, keeping things consistent, and giving users control. We've seen that the field of UX Design is constantly evolving, but with a solid understanding of the principles and a little bit of humor, we can create interfaces that will make users smile from ear to ear.

To all the future UX Designers, don't forget that users come first and have fun while you're at it. To all the users out there, if you ever come across an interface that's not quite right, just remember that a team of designers and developers are working hard to make it better. And always, always remember to share your feedback, it helps us make things even better! So, let's keep the quest for exceptional interfaces going, with a smile on our faces and a skip in our steps.

20

THE ANATOMY ADVENTURE OF UI ELEMENTS

Design is a laugh riot of a word. People believe it's all about the looks, but that's just the tip of the iceberg. Scratch beneath the surface and it's really about the performance!

U I design may seem like a dry and boring topic, but trust me, it's anything but in fact, the world of UI design is filled with all sorts of wacky and wild elements that can make your head spin. From buttons to text fields, from icons to modals, the UI landscape is a veritable jungle of design decisions waiting to be made.

But before I dive into the nitty-gritty of UI design, let's first take a moment to appreciate the beauty of the elements that make up the user interface. These elements are the building blocks of any good design, and without them, your users would be lost in a sea of confusion and despair.

So, without further ado, let's take a tour of the most important UI elements and see what makes them tick.

The Grid of Madness

Once upon a time, in a land far, far away, there lived a group of UI designers. They were known throughout the land for their exceptional design skills and their ability to create beautiful and user-friendly interfaces. However, there was one problem that they faced on a daily basis: the dreaded task of creating grids and layouts for their designs.

You see, the UI designers were a bit of a lazy bunch. They didn't particularly enjoy the tedious and time-consuming task of aligning elements and making sure everything was perfectly spaced. But alas, it was a necessary evil, and so they trudged on, day after day.

One day, a brilliant young designer named Flexy McFlaxson had an idea. "Why not create a system that would make creating grids and layouts a breeze?" he thought to himself. And so, Flexy set out to create the ultimate tool for UI designers everywhere.

He began by gathering all of the best practices for creating grids and layouts. He studied the works of the greats, such as Bootstrap and Foundation, and even consulted with the wise old Grid Wizard. He took all of this knowledge and combined it with his own unique ideas and created the Flexbox Funhouse.

The Flexbox Funhouse was a magical tool that allowed designers to easily create grids and layouts with just a few clicks of a button. It was a hit among the UI designer community and soon, everyone was using it. The tedious task of creating grids and layouts was a thing of the past.

But not everyone was happy with Flexy's creation. The Grid of Chaos, a powerful and malevolent entity, was angered by the success of the Flexbox Funhouse. He saw it as a threat to his own existence and vowed to destroy it.

The Grid of Chaos began spreading lies and rumors about the Flexbox Funhouse, claiming that it was unstable and unreliable. He even went so far as to hack into the system and cause it to malfunction.

The UI designers were confused and worried. They didn't know who to believe or what to do. But Flexy was not one to be defeated so easily. He rallied his fellow designers and together, they set out to defeat the Grid of Chaos and restore the Flexbox Funhouse to its former glory.

They battled fiercely, using all of their knowledge of grids and layouts to outsmart the Grid of Chaos. In the end, they emerged victorious and the Flexbox Funhouse was once again the go-to tool for creating grids and layouts.

And so, the UI designers lived happily ever after, free from the tedious task of creating grids and layouts. They all lived in Flexbox Funhouse and use it for every project.

The story is good but what the heck is a grid?

Grids. They're the backbone of UI/UX design, the bread and butter of layout, and the glue that holds it all together. But let's be honest, they're not exactly the most exciting topic in the world. I mean, sure, they're important and all, but they're not exactly the kind of thing that gets your blood pumping.

Well, that's where I come in. My goal is to make grids exciting. Or at least, as exciting as grids can be. First off, let's talk about what grids are. Simply put, a grid is a system of horizontal and vertical lines that divide a layout into a series of equal-sized cells. These cells can then be used to organize and position elements on a page. Think of it like a giant game of Tetris, except instead of trying to fit blocks into a specific shape, you're trying to fit elements into specific cells.

Now, you might be thinking, "But wait, isn't that just a table? Like the kind you use in Excel?" And you would be correct. Grids and tables are very similar. But while tables are used to organize and present data, grids are used to organize and present elements on a page. And while tables are typically used in spreadsheets, grids are used in everything from websites to mobile apps to print design.

But why are grids so important in UI/UX design? Well, for one, they help create a sense of order and structure on a page. When elements are arranged in a grid, it makes it easier for users to understand and navigate the layout. It also helps create a sense of consistency, which is important for creating a cohesive design.

Grids also help with alignment and spacing. By using a grid, elements can be aligned and spaced in a consistent manner, which makes for a more aesthetically pleasing design. And when elements are aligned and spaced correctly, it makes it easier for users to scan and read the content.

But wait, there's more! Grids can also be used to create different types of layouts. For example, a grid with a single column can be used for a simple, linear layout. A grid with multiple columns can be used for a more complex, multi-dimensional layout. And grids can also be used to create different types of typography, such as a grid of headlines or a grid of body text.

So, there you have it. Grids are the unsung heroes of UI/UX design. They may not be the most exciting topic, but they're certainly important ones. And now, you can impress your friends and colleagues with your newfound knowledge of grids. Or, you know, you could just use it to create better designs. Either way, it's a win-win.

Whether simple or complex, all grids have some common parts:

Format: The format, is where all the design magic happens. Think of it as the stage for your design performance. Like a Broadway show, the format sets the scene. In a traditional paper book, the format is the page - where all the words and pictures come together to tell a story. But in the wild world of the web, the format is the size of the browser window - the ultimate stage for your design to shine like a star in a one-browser window show.

Margins: Margins are like the fancy pants of your UI Design. They're the sassy little negative space that keeps all your content looking neat and tidy. Think of them as the bouncers of your layout, keeping everything in line and preventing any unwanted elements from creeping in. Without margins, your UI Design would be like a wild party with no rules - chaos and confusion everywhere. So, embrace those margins, give them a little love, and watch as your design transforms into a beautiful, well-organized masterpiece.

Columns and Alleys: Columns, the fancy crackers of the grid, hold everything together. And the alleys, the spaces in between those crackers, are like the fancy jam that makes everything come together. Together, they'll take up the entire width of your screen and make your design look like a fancy feast fit for royalty.

Modules: Modules are like little cubicles for your design elements, where they can sit and chit-chat about the latest trends and layouts. Think of them as the office water cooler of UI design, where columns and rows come together to form the perfect little gossiping spot for your design elements. So go ahead, let your design elements mingle and network in their little modules, who knows, they might just come up with the next big thing in UI design.

Now buckle up, because we're about to dive into the four standard layout grids: the manuscript grid, the column grid, the modular grid, and the baseline grid. These grids are like pieces of a puzzle, and when combined in different ways, they can create some truly unique and awe-inspiring layouts. So, when might you use each of these grids? Well, that's what we're about to find out. So, grab a pen and paper, because it's time to take some notes and get ready for a layout grid extravaganza!

Manuscript Grid: Step right up, folks! Allow me to introduce you to the MVP of grid structures: the infamous single-column grid, also known as the 'manuscript grid.' Think of it as a giant rectangle that takes up most of the space in your design, like a house for all your text to live in. And let's be real, who doesn't love a good text block party?

But don't be fooled, this grid ain't just for the written word, throw in some images and you'll have a real shindig on your hands. Now, I know what you're thinking, "But wait, doesn't the name suggest it's just for the printed page?" Well, let me tell you, this grid has been around since the days of quill and parchment and it's still going strong. So, if you're looking for a tried and true, classic grid structure, look no further than the single-column grid, the life of the layout design party.

Multicolumn Grid: I'm about to drop some serious grid knowledge on you. Introducing the multi-talented, the jack-of-all-trades, the multicolumn grid (drumroll please). As the name suggests, this bad boy doesn't mess around with just one measly column.' It's got multiple

columns, like a buffet of layout options. And the more columns you add, the more flexibility you have. Think of it like a choose-your-own-adventure book, but for design.

These grids are particularly handy for layouts that have a lot of different types of information that don't fit nicely together like puzzle pieces. With a multicolumn grid, you can create zones for different types of content, like a dedicated column for illustrations, or one for captions. It's like having your own personal assistant for organizing your layout. So, if you're looking to up your grid game, go for the multicolumn grid and watch your layout soar to new heights.

Modular Grid: Modular grids are like the superhero of layout design - they swoop in and save the day when a simple column grid just won't cut it. With their flexible formats and ability to create a complex hierarchy, they're the ultimate control freaks (in a good way). Each module is like a mini powerhouse, containing just the right amount of information to get the job done. And when things get really tough, they can team up with their neighboring modules to form unstoppable blocks of awesomeness. So the next time you're facing a layout crisis, call in the modular grid squad and watch the magic happen.

Baseline Grid: A baseline grid is like the invisible ruler of the design world. It's the secret sauce that keeps everything in line and makes sure that everything is where it's supposed to be. Think of it like a trusty sidekick that always has your back when you're laying out elements on the page. It's kind of like writing on a ruled piece of paper, except instead of making sure your handwriting is straight, it makes sure that the bottom of each line of text (its baseline) is perfectly aligned with the vertical spacing. Basically, it's like a superhero that saves the day when you're laying out elements on the page and you're not sure if something is missing a row of space. So, if you want your design to look like it was made by a pro, make sure to use a baseline grid! Just don't forget to thank it for all its hard work.

Continuing our journey in Grid Park... Once upon a time, in the land of digital product design, grids were considered nothing more than a boring, rigid structures that only served to confine the creativity of designers. But then, a new hero emerged on the scene: interaction design.

Interaction design changed the way we think about grids. Suddenly, grids weren't just a tool for keeping things in line, they were a tool for creating a seamless and intuitive experience for users, no matter what device they were using.

You see, with the rise of smartwatches and ultra-wide TV screens, the world of digital design had become a chaotic place. People were using all sorts of different devices to interact with products, and designers were struggling to keep up. But interaction design was here to save the day.

Interaction design is fluid and doesn't have a fixed size because people are using different types of devices to interact with the product. Despite screen size, design-ers must organize content in the most intuitive and easy-to-follow way. One approach to achieving this is to use a layout grid system. A layout grid is preferable for interactive design because it defines the underlying structure of a design and how each component responds to different breakpoints. This type of grid is faster and easier to design for multiple screens and resolutions.

But why is a layout grid system so important? Well, let me tell you. Grid systems in digital product design organize el-ements on the page and connect spaces. A grid system improves the quality of a design (functionally and aesthetically) and the efficiency of the design process in several ways:

First, grids create clarity and consistency. A grid is a foundation for order in a design. Proportion, rhythm, white space and hierarchy are all design characteristics that directly affect cognitive speed. Grids create and enforce the consistency of these elements throughout an interface. An effective grid guides the eye, making it easier and more pleasant to scan objects on the screen.

This is especially important in digital products because they are functional, meaning that people use the products to complete specific tasks, such as sending a message, booking a hotel room, or hailing a car ride. Consistency helps the viewer understand where to find the next piece of information or what step to take next.

Second, grids improve design comprehension. The human brain makes judgments in a fraction of a second. A design that is poorly put together will make the product seem less usable and trustworthy. Grids connect and reinforce the visual hierarchy of the design by providing a set of rules, such as where elements should go in the layout.

Third, grids make responsive. Responsive design is no longer a luxury, but rather a necessity because people experience apps and websites on devices with a broad range of screens. This means that designers can no longer build for a single device's screen. The multidevice landscape forces designers to think in terms of dynamic grid systems, instead of fixed widths. Using a grid creates a consistent experience across multiple devices with different screen sizes.

Fourth, grids quicken the design process. Grids enable designers to manage the proportions between UI elements, such as spacing and margins. This helps to create pixel-perfect designs from the start and avoid timely reworking caused by incorrect adjustments.

And last but not least, grids facilitate collaboration. Grids make it easier for designers to collaborate on designs by providing a plan for where to place elements. Grid systems help to decouple work on interface design because multiple designers can work on different parts of the layout, knowing that their work will be seamlessly integrated and consistent.

When it comes to designing with grids, it can sometimes feel like trying to tame a wild beast. But fear not, my fellow designers, for I have compiled a list of best practices to help you navigate the treacherous waters of grid design.

First things first, let's talk about selecting the right grid for you. "How many columns do I need?" is the eternal question of every designer. The answer, my friends, is that it depends on your design needs. Sure, the 12-column grid is a popular choice, but if 8 columns are all you need, then don't waste your time on those extra 4 columns. Sketch out your possible layouts and let the content define the grid, not the other way around.

Next up, consider the constraints on your design. If most of your users are using a specific device, like a phone, make sure to design with that constraint in mind. It's all about focusing on what's important to your users. And speaking of important, don't forget to add more visual weight to important elements by stretching them across multiple columns.

But don't get too comfortable in the grid, sometimes it's good to step outside and break the rules. Just make sure you know what you're doing and don't break the visual hierarchy or impair the user experience. And don't forget about both horizontal and vertical spacing. Consistency is key when it comes to grids.

And, last but not least, let's talk about the MVP of grids, the baseline grid. This little guy is a superhero when it comes to horizontal alignment and hierarchy. Just make sure to align UI design elements to a baseline and you'll be good to go.

And, for all, you mobile designers out there, don't forget to optimize your grids for those tiny screens. A tile layout grid is a great option for limited space and remember, less is more with mobile grids.

Designing with a grid can be a wild ride, but by following these best practices, you'll be able to tame that beast and create a consistent, organized design.

In conclusion, grid systems are like the hot sauce of design - they add a little bit of spice and make everything come together perfectly. But, just like hot sauce, too much can be overwhelming and ruin the whole dish. So, practice makes perfect when it comes to using grids in your designs. Like Josef, Muller-Brockmann said, "The grid system is an aid, not a guarantee." It's an art that requires practice, so don't be afraid to experiment and find your own unique style. And remember, a little bit of grid goes a long way.

Button, Button, Magic Button!

Buttons, buttons, buttons. They may seem like small, insignificant pieces of a user interface, but they are actually the unsung heroes of the digital world. They are the gatekeepers, the decision-makers, and the facilitators of action. Without buttons, how would we navigate through our favorite apps? How would we send that "I'm going home or I love you" message or tweet? How would we even turn on our phones? The answer is simple: we wouldn't.

Buttons come in all shapes and sizes, each with its own unique purpose and functionality. There are the standard round buttons, the square buttons, the rectangular buttons, and even the elusive oval button (which is like a unicorn of the button world). Each button serves a specific function, whether it's to submit a form, navigate to a new page, or initiate a call to action.

Buttons can also be designed in various ways, with different colors, gradients, and text. Some buttons are sleek and min- imalistic, while others are bold and eye-catching. And let's not forget about the hover effect, that subtle yet satisfying animation that occurs when you hover your cursor over a button. It's like a little surprise party for your fingers.

Buttons can also be customized to match the overall aes- thetic and branding of a website or app. They can be made to match the color scheme of a website or even be designed to look like a physical button, complete with a shiny metallic texture and a satisfying "click" sound when pressed.

Buttons can also be used in unexpected ways, such as in the form of a game or interactive experience. Have you ever played a game where you had to click on a button as quickly as possible? It's like a digital version of a carnival game, and just as addictive. And let's not forget about the "easter egg" button, hidden away in a corner of a website, waiting to be discovered and pressed, revealing a hidden message or surprise.

As a professional designer, I must admit that I have never given much thought to the humble button. Sure, I've clicked on them a million times, but I never really stopped to consider the different types that exist in the world of UI design. But as it turns out, there is a whole world of buttons out there, each with their own unique purpose and design.

Let's start with the most basic of all buttons: the CTA (call-to-action) button. This is the button that you see everywhere, urging you to "Sign Up," "Buy Now," or "Learn More." It's usually the largest button on the page, and it's there to entice you to take action.

Next up is the Text button. This is a simple button that contains only text, usually in small font sizes. It's often used as a secondary action, such as "Cancel" or "Back."

The Ghost button is a more modern take on the Text button. It's a button that is transparent, with only the text visible. This gives it a sleek and minimalist look, making it perfect for modern websites and apps.

The Dropdown button is a button that, when clicked, expands to reveal a menu of options. This is often used for navigation or settings.

The Floating Action Button (FAB) is a unique button that floats above the rest of the content on the page. It's usually used for a primary action, such as "New," "Create," or "Share."

The Hamburger button is a button that is shaped like a hamburger (three horizontal lines stacked on top of each other). When clicked, it expands to reveal a menu of options. This is often used for navigation in mobile apps.

The Plus button is a button that is shaped like a plus sign (+). It's often used to add something, such as a new item or a new contact.

The Expendable button is a button that, when clicked, expands to reveal more options. This is often used for advanced settings or options.

The Share button is a button that, when clicked, opens a menu of options for sharing content on social media or other platforms.

Finally, we have the Raised button. This is a button that is raised above the rest of the content on the page, giving it a 3D look. It's often used for important actions, such as "Save" or "Submit."

As you can see, there are many different types of UI buttons out there, each with its own unique design and purpose. Whether you're a designer or just a user, it's important to understand the different types of buttons and how they can be used to enhance the user experience. So next time you're clicking on a button, take a moment to appreciate the design and functionality of this humble but powerful element of UI design.

Designing the perfect button in UI design is a delicate art. It may seem like a simple task, but there are many factors to consider when creating a button that is both functional and aesthetically pleasing.

First and foremost, let's talk about size. Size is crucial when it comes to buttons. A button that is too small can be difficult to press, and a button that is too large can take up too much space on the screen. The perfect button size will depend on the device and platform you are designing for. For example, a button on a mobile device should be larger than a button on a desktop website.

When it comes to mobile design, a button should be at least 44px x 44px. This size allows for easy tapping on small screens and ensures that the button is visible on high-resolution devices. For desktop design, a button should be at least 30px x 30px. This size allows for easy clicking and ensures that the button is visible on large screens.

But size isn't the only factor to consider when designing a button. Another important aspect is padding. Padding refers to the space between the button and the surrounding elements. Padding is crucial for creating a button that stands out and is easy to press. A button with too little padding can be difficult to tap or click, while a button with too much padding can take up too much space on the screen.

The perfect padding for a button will depend on the size of the button and the surrounding elements. A general rule of thumb is to use at least 8px of padding around the button. This allows for enough space for the user to tap or click the button while also ensuring that the button stands out from the surrounding elements.

Buttons should also have enough space between them, otherwise, users might accidentally press the wrong button. A good rule of thumb is to use at least 8px of space between buttons. This ensures that users can easily tap or click the correct button without accidentally selecting the wrong one.

Another important aspect of button design is the color. The color of the button should be contrasting with the background and the text color should be readable.

Bright colors such as red and green are commonly used to indicate positive or negative actions.

In addition, the button should have a hover effect that indicates that the button is clickable and a pressed effect that indicates that the button has been clicked. These effects can be subtle, such as a slight change in color or a slight change in the button's shape.

Designing the perfect button in UI design requires a great deal of attention to detail. Size, padding, color, hover, and pressed effects should all be carefully considered to create a button that is functional and visually pleasing. Remember to always test your buttons on different devices and platforms to ensure that they are easy to press and easy to see.

As a professional UI designer, I can attest to the importance of button placement in the overall design of a website or application. But let's be real, it's not always easy to decide where those little guys should go. It can be a real button-placement conundrum.

First, let's start with the basics. The most important button on any website or app is the one that says, "Buy Now", "Sign Up" or "I Want More Chocolates." (Okay, maybe not the last one, but you get the idea.) These buttons are the ultimate goal of the user's journey and should be prominently displayed, usually above the fold and in a contrasting color to the rest of the design.

Next, we have the navigation buttons. These are the buttons that allow the user to move around the website or app, such as "Home," "About Us," and "Contact Us." These should be placed in a consistent location on every page, such as at the top or in the sidebar, to make it easy for users to find them.

But what about the other buttons? The ones that say, "Learn More," "Watch Video," or "Download Now"? These are important too, but they don't need to be front and center. In fact, if they are too prominent, they can distract from the main goal of the website or app. These buttons should be placed in logical locations, such as next to the corresponding content or in a call-to-action section.

And then there are the buttons that nobody really wants to click on, like "Terms of Service" or "Privacy Policy." These buttons are necessary, but they shouldn't be in the way. The best place for these buttons is in a footer or in a drop-down menu. That way, they're easily accessible, but they don't take up valuable real estate on the page.

But wait, there's more! What about mobile devices? The placement of buttons on a small screen is a whole different ballgame. Buttons need to be larger and spaced farther apart to make them easy to tap with a finger. And forget about those tiny buttons in the corner of the screen - they're just asking to be accidentally tapped.

So, as you can see, button placement is not just about aesthetics, it's about making the user's journey as easy and seamless as possible. And let's face it, it's also about preventing accidental clicks on the "Privacy Policy" button (because who really wants to read that?). But remember, when in doubt, just ask yourself, "Where would I expect to find this button?" And then put it there. And if all else fails, just put a cowbell button on there. Because who doesn't love chocolates?

In conclusion, buttons are a vital component of UI design and should not be taken lightly. They are the gatekeepers to all the functionality and features of a website or app, and without them, we would be lost in a sea of confusion and frustration. They are the unsung heroes of the digital world, tirelessly working behind the scenes to make our lives easier and more enjoyable. So, next time you click on a button, take a moment to appreciate the hard work and dedication that went into making it possible. And remember, without buttons, we would all be stuck in the Stone Age, trying to navigate our way around with a chisel and a rock. So, let's give a round of applause to the buttons, the backbone of our digital world. Buttons, we salute you!

The Times New Roman of a Joke: How to Use Typography to Punch up Your Punchlines in UI Design

Ah, typography. The bane of every designer's existence. The history of typography in UI design is a long and winding one, full of twists and turns, and more than a few jokes along the way. But before we dive into the nitty-gritty of it all, let's start with the basics: what exactly is typography?

At its core, typography is the art and technique of arranging type to make written language legible, readable and appealing when displayed. This can include things like choosing the right font, adjusting the size and spacing of letters and words, and even playing with color and other design elements to create a cohesive and visually pleasing layout.

Now, let's fast forward to the early days of UI design. Back in the days of early computers, the options for typography were pretty limited. Most computer screens could only display a handful of basic fonts, and there wasn't much room for creativity or experimentation. But as technology progressed and screens became more advanced, designers began to push the boundaries of what was possible with typography in UI design.

One of the first major breakthroughs in this field came with the introduction of web fonts in the late 1990s. Before this, designers were limited to using the same basic fonts that were pre-installed on every computer. But with web fonts, designers could now choose from a much wider range of typefaces, allowing them to create more unique and visually interesting layouts.

As technology continued to evolve, so too did the possibilities for typography in UI design. Today, designers have access to an almost endless array of fonts, sizes, and design elements, giving them the ability to create truly striking and engaging layouts.

But it's not just about the technical side of things. Good typography in UI design also requires a keen eye for aesthetics and a deep understanding of how people interact with the text. After all, the ultimate goal of any UI design is to make the interface as easy to use and as intuitive as possible, and typography plays a huge role in that.

Typography, the art, and technique of arranging type in order to make written language legible, readable, and appealing when displayed, plays a crucial role in UI design. It's the backbone of any interface, the foundation upon which all other design elements are built. Think of it as the meat and potatoes of design, the bread, and butter of the user experience. Without proper typography, an interface would be like a salad without lettuce, a cake without frosting, or a comedy show without jokes. It just wouldn't be complete.

Typography is the first thing that users notice when they interact with an interface, and it sets the tone for the entire experience. It's like a first impression, and we all know how important those are. A well-designed typography system can make users feel calm and reassured, while a poorly designed one can make them feel confused and frustrated. Imagine trying to read a menu in a restaurant with tiny, cramped font and no spacing between lines. You'd probably just give up and order something you don't really want, just to get out of there.

But typography isn't just about making text legible, it's also about making it aesthetically pleasing. A good typography system should be visually appealing and create a sense of harmony with the rest of the design. Think of it like a symphony, with different typefaces, sizes, and colors working together to create a cohesive whole. Just like a good symphony should be easy to listen to, a good typography system should be easy to read.

And just like a symphony, typography can also be used to create emotion. A bold, sans-serif typeface can evoke a sense of confidence and authority, while a delicate, serif typeface can evoke a sense of elegance and sophistication. And let's not forget about the power of humor. A playful typeface can add a touch of levity to an interface, making it more approachable and friendly.

When it comes to typography, there are a plethora of different elements to consider. First and foremost, there are fonts and typefaces. Now, you may be thinking, "aren't those the same thing?"

Well, my dear reader, allow me to enlighten you. Fonts refer to the technical aspect of typography - the actual file that is used to create the text. Typefaces, on the other hand, are the design aspect of typography - the visual appearance of the text. So, when you're choosing a font for your project, you're selecting the typeface as well. But let's not get too caught up in semantics - the important thing is to choose a font that is legible and appropriate for the project at hand.

Next up, we have consistency. This element is key when it comes to creating a cohesive design. It's important to have consistency in the font, typeface, and overall layout. Imagine if every paragraph in a book was in a different font - it would be a mess! And let's not even get started on the horror show that would be if every sentence had a different alignment. Consistency is like the glue that holds a design together - without it, the design would fall apart.

Another important element in typography is white space. Now, you may be thinking, "white space? But isn't that just empty space?" Well, yes and no. White space is the empty space around and between elements in a design. It's important to use white space effectively, as it can help to create a sense of balance and hierarchy. Think of it like a pause in a song - it gives the audience a moment to breathe before the next verse begins.

Speaking of hierarchy, let's talk about alignment. Alignment refers to how text is aligned within a design. There are four basic types of alignment: left, center, right, and justified. Each type of alignment can be used to create a different visual effect and to help establish hierarchy within a design.

For example, if you want to create a sense of importance for a particular piece of text, you might center-align it.

And, finally, we have color and contrast. Color is an incredibly powerful tool in design, and it can be used to create a specific mood or feeling. Contrast, on the other hand, refers to the difference in lightness and darkness between elements in a design. It's important to use contrast effectively, as it can help to make the text more legible and to create a sense of hierarchy. So, when you're working on a design project, don't just choose colors willy-nilly - think about how they will work together and how they will create contrast.

When it comes to using typography in UI design, there are a few key things to keep in mind. First and foremost, choosing the right font can make or break your design. You want to pick a font that is easy to read and pleasing to the eye. But don't be afraid to have a little fun with it too! After all, who says the design has to be all business all the time? A little whimsy can go a long way in making your design stand out.

Formatting is key. You want to make sure your text is easy to scan and understand. This means using headings and subheadings to break up your text and make it easy to navigate. And don't forget about white space! This is the area around and between your text, and it's crucial for making your design look clean and uncluttered.

Hierarchy is also important when it comes to typography in UI design. This refers to the order and importance of elements in your design. For example, your headings should be larger and bolder than your body text, to indicate that they are more important. And don't forget about line height! This is the space between lines of text, and it can make a big difference in how easy your text is to read.

Finally, don't forget about letter spacing and word spacing. These are the spaces between individual letters and words, respectively. They might seem like small details, but they can have a big impact on how easy your text is to read. A little extra space between letters and words can make a big difference in how easy your text is to scan.

In short, there's a lot to keep in mind when it comes to using typography in UI design. But by focusing on things like font choice, formatting, white space, hierarchy, line height, letter spacing, and word spacing, you can create a design that is easy to read, pleasing to the eye, and sure to stand out from the crowd. So go forth and design away! And remember, a little humor never hurt anyone. So don't be afraid to have a little fun with it!

A Colorful Adventure in UI Design

When it comes to UI design, colors are like the spices in a dish - they can make or break the overall experience. But unlike spices, there's no recipe for the perfect color scheme. It's all about experimenting and finding what works for your specific project.

First things first, let's talk about color theory. This is the science of how colors interact and how they affect us emotionally and psychologically. It's like a big game of emotional Tetris - you have to figure out how to fit all the different colors together in a way that makes sense and evokes the desired emotions.

For example, blue is often associated with trust and professionalism, while red is associated with energy and excitement. So, if you're designing a website for a bank, you might want to use a lot of blues, but if you're designing a website for a concert venue, you might want to use a lot of red.

But it's not just about choosing the right colors, it's also about how you use them. If you use too much of one color, it can be overwhelming and jarring. It's like trying to eat a whole jar of pickles - it might sound good in theory, but in reality, it's just too much.

Now, how do you find the perfect balance? Well, it's all about experimentation. Try different color schemes and see how they make you feel. Does it evoke the desired emotions? Does it make the interface easy to use? Does it look good on different devices and in different lighting conditions?

One of the most important things to keep in mind is accessibility. Not everyone can see colors the same way, so it's important to make sure your color scheme is accessible to all. This means using high-contrast colors and making sure there's enough contrast between different elements on the page.

Enough with the serious stuff, let's talk about some of the more fun and quirky ways to use colors in UI design. Have you ever heard of the "rainbow effect"? This is when you use a bunch of different colors in a random and chaotic way. It's like a unicorn threw up all over your interface but in a good way.

Another fun idea is to use colors to create different moods. For example, you could use cool colors (like blue and green) to create a calming and soothing atmosphere, or warm colors (like red and orange) to create a sense of energy and excitement.

And finally, don't be afraid to think outside the box. Just because everyone else is using blue and green doesn't mean you have to. Why not try using pink and purple? It might sound crazy, but it could end up being the perfect color scheme for your project.

In conclusion, colors are an important part of UI design and can greatly affect the overall user experience. But it's not just about choosing the right colors, it's also about how you use them and finding the perfect balance. So don't be afraid to experiment and have fun with it - who knows, you might just end up creating the next unicorn-inspired color scheme.

Gradients Gone Wild

Let's not be so quick to dismiss these colorful little buggers. Sure, they may seem like a frivolous addition to your design, but they can actually be quite useful.

First off, let's talk about what gradients are. In layman's terms, they're basically a blend of two or more colors that seamlessly transition into one another. Think of it like a smoothie, but with colors instead of fruit. And just like a smoothie, you can mix and match different colors to create a unique and visually appealing design.

But why use gradients in your UI design? Well, for one, they can add depth and dimension to your design. By using gradients, you can create the illusion of depth, making your design look more three-dimensional and realistic. This can be especially useful for creating buttons, icons, and other interactive elements that you want to stand out.

Another benefit of using gradients is that they can add a sense of movement and energy to your design. By using gradients that transition from light to dark or from warm to cool colors, you can create the illusion of movement and give your design a sense of dynamic energy. This can be especially useful for creating animations and other interactive elements that you want to look lively and engaging.

But let's not forget the most important use of gradients in UI design: they're just plain fun to play with! Who doesn't love playing with colors and seeing what cool combinations you can come up with? And let's be real, sometimes a design just needs a little pop of color to make it feel more alive and interesting.

So, the next time you're working on a UI design and you're tempted to dismiss gradients as unnecessary, remember that they can add depth, dimension, movement, and even a little bit of fun to your design. Plus, they're like a smoothie for your eyes. And who doesn't love a good smoothie?

But of course, it's worth noting that everything should be used in moderation. Gradients can be overwhelming and too much of them can make the design look cluttered. So, use them wisely and don't overdo them.

In the end, gradients can be an important and useful tool in your UI design arsenal. So, don't be afraid to experiment with different colors and transitions to see what kind of visual magic you can create. And remember, when it comes to gradients, a little bit can go a long way.

Let There Be Shadows

When it comes to UI design, shadows can be a tricky thing to master. You want to create depth and dimension, but not so much that it becomes overwhelming or confusing for the user. So, how do you strike the perfect balance?

First, let's talk about what shadows do in UI design. Essentially, they create the illusion of depth and dimension by adding a sense of elevation and movement to elements on the screen. Think about it like this: if everything on your screen was flat, it would look like a cardboard cutout. But by adding shadows, you can make it feel like those elements are popping out at you.

But it's not just about adding shadows from hands like Spiderman. You have to be strategic about where and how you use them. For example, if you have a button that you want to stand out, you might add a subtle drop shadow to make it appear as if it's hovering above the rest of the elements on the screen. On the other hand, if you have a section of your screen that you want to recede into the background, you might add some softer, more diffuse shadows to make it appear as if it's further away.

Of course, there's a fine line between creating depth and dimension and making your UI look cluttered and chaotic. So, how do you avoid crossing that line?

One key is to stick to a consistent style of shadows throughout your design. If you're using drop shadows on buttons, make sure that they're all the same size and intensity. If you're using diffuse shadows to create depth, make sure that they're all in the same direction. This will help create a cohesive look and feel that doesn't feel overwhelming.

Another thing to keep in mind is to not overdo it. A little bit of shadow goes a long way, so don't feel like you have to add shadows to every single element on the screen. In fact, sometimes the absence of shadows can be just as powerful as their presence. So, don't be afraid to leave some elements shadow-free to create a sense of contrast and balance.

But perhaps the most important thing to remember when it comes to shadows in UI design is to have fun with it! After all, it's not rocket science (or is it?!) Play around with different styles and intensities of shadows and see what looks and feels good to you. And, most importantly, don't be afraid to make mistakes. Because let's face it, even the greatest shadow masters have had their fair share of missteps.

So, go forth and create some killer shadow effects in your UI design. And remember, with great shadow power comes great shadow responsibility!

Forms of Persuasion

Ladies and gentlemen gather 'round because it's time to talk about the boring topic of forms in UI design! But don't worry, because I'm not just any ol' boring writer, I'm a designer, and I'm here to make this topic as exciting as a rollercoaster ride through a cheese factory (okay, maybe not that exciting, but bear with me here).

So, what the heck are forms in UI design? Well, imagine you're trying to buy a new pair of shoes online. You click on the "add to cart" button, and then BAM! A group of boxes pops up asking for your shoe size, shipping address, and credit card information. That, my friends, is a form.

But forms aren't just for buying shoes, they're used for all sorts of things, like creating a new account, filling out a survey, or even just sending an email. They're like the unsung heroes of the internet, without them, we'd all be stuck trying to communicate with our thumbs via text message (and let's be real, nobody wants to see that).

But why are forms so important in UI design? Well, for starters, they're the gatekeepers of information. Without forms, websites would be a free-for-all of spam and misinformation. Plus, they help make sure you're getting the information you need from your users. Imagine trying to run an online store without a form to collect shipping information, you'd be sending shoes to random people in Timbuktu (which sounds like a fun party game, but not so great for business).

But let's not forget about the user experience. Forms can be a real pain in the butt if they're not designed properly. You know the feeling; you're trying to buy a new pair of shoes and you get stuck in a never-ending loop of "please enter a valid email address" messages. That's why it's important to make forms as user-friendly as possible, like giving clear instructions, using error messages sparingly, and making sure the form is easy to fill out on a mobile device (because let's be real, who wants to fill out a form on a tiny phone screen?).

Now, I know what you're thinking, "this is all well and good, but can't you make it a little more exciting?" Well, I'll tell you what, I'll make it a little game. I'll give you a list of forms, and you have to guess what they're used for. Are you ready?

A form asking for your name, email address, and password.

A form asking for your favorite ice cream flavor, toppings, and whether you prefer a cone or a cup.

A form asking for your credit card information, shipping address, and a special discount code.

If you guessed 1. creating a new account, 2. a survey for an ice cream shop, and 3. buying a new pair of shoes, you're correct! And if you didn't, well, don't worry, forms aren't for everyone (but they are necessary for the internet to function properly).

So, forms may not be the most exciting topic in the world, but they're important for keeping the internet organized, secure, and user-friendly. And remember, next time you're filling out a form, think of it as a fun game of "guess what I'm trying to do.

Remember, form is the barrier that separates the casual browser from the dedicated user. Think of it like a bouncer at a fancy club. You can't just walk in without showing ID, and a form is the digital version of that ID. So, it's crucial that your form is designed in a way that makes it easy for users to fill out, while also being secure and efficient.

Now, before we dive into the nitty-gritty of form design, I want to remind you of one important rule: KISS. Keep it simple, stupid. This applies to forms as well. Don't overcomplicate things by adding unnecessary fields or making the layout too confusing. Keep it simple, and your users will thank you.

Now, let's talk about the layout of your form. Think of it like a sandwich. You have your bread, the top and bottom of the form, the filling, the fields, and the buttons. The bread is the frame that holds everything together, and the filling is the juicy meat of the form. Just like a sandwich, your form should have a clear structure that is easy to understand.

The bread, or the top and bottom of the form, should contain the main information and actions. This could be a title, a call to action, or even a navigation menu. The filling, or the fields and buttons, should be arranged in a logical order, with the most important fields at the top and the least important at the bottom. And just like a sandwich, make sure your form isn't too bulky or overloaded with too many fields.

Next up, let's talk about the fields themselves. These are the heart and soul of your form, and they should be designed with care. First and foremost, make sure the labels are clear and easy to read. Use simple language and avoid jargon. Also, make sure the fields are aligned and have a consistent size and style. This will make it easier for users to fill out the form, and it will also make it look more professional.

Another important aspect of fields is the input type. This is the type of data the field is meant to collect, such as text, numbers, or email addresses. Make sure you use the correct input type for each field, and also, provide clear instructions on what kind of data should be entered. For example, don't just label a field "email," and tell the user to enter their "email address."

And finally, let's talk about the buttons. These are the cherry on top of your form. Without them, your users won't be able to submit the form, and you'll be left with a bunch of incomplete sandwiches. Make sure your buttons are clear and easy to find. Use contrasting colors and make them big enough to be easily tapped or clicked. And most importantly, make sure the text on the button is clear and easy to understand. Don't use "submit" if you want the user to "send" the form.

Designing a perfect form in UI design is not rocket science. It's all about keeping it simple, having a clear structure, and paying.

In conclusion, forms are like that one annoying relative at a family gathering. They ask a lot of questions, they never seem to be satisfied, and they always seem to be hanging around. But just like that annoying relative, forms serve a crucial role in UI design. They allow users to input information, and without them, we would be lost in a world of confusion and chaos. So, next time you're filling out a form and feeling frustrated, just remember that it's for the greater good. And if all else fails, just think of it as a game of 20 questions with a computer.

The Icon-ic

Let's face it, folks. We live in a world where we're constantly bombarded with information. Everywhere we look, there's a screen trying to grab our attention. And let's be real, as much as we love scrolling through our social media feeds, sometimes it can feel like a never-ending cycle of cat videos and political memes. So, how do we navigate through this digital chaos? Icons, my friends. Icons are the tour guides of the digital world. They're the ones that save us from confusion and guide us to the information we need.

But why are icons so important in UI design? Well, first of all, they're like the ultimate shorthand. Think about it, when you see a little envelope icon, you know it's probably an email. A little speech bubble? Probably a message. A little magnifying glass? Searching for something. It's like a secret code that only the initiated can understand. And let's be real, who doesn't love feeling like they're part of an exclusive club?

But icons aren't just there to make us feel cool. They also help us process information faster. Our brains are wired to recognize and process visual information more quickly than text. So, when we see an icon, our brains are like "Oh, I know what that means! I don't have to read a bunch of text to figure it out." It's like the difference between reading a book and watching a movie. You get the same information, but one is way faster and more fun.

But perhaps the most important reason icons are crucial in UI design is that they help create a sense of consistency and organization. Imagine if every app or website had different icons for the same function. It would be like trying to navigate a foreign country where everyone speaks a different language. It would be like John Wick is chasing you and you're confused about this new country where to go. But with icons, there's a sense of familiarity. We know what to expect and where to find what we need. It's like a digital roadmap that guides us through the digital landscape.

Now, I know what you're thinking. "But wait, icons aren't just cute little pictures. They're serious business!" And you're right. Icons are serious business. But that doesn't mean they can't be fun too. In fact, the best icons are the ones that are both functional and visually appealing. It's like having your cake and eating it too. And who doesn't love cake?

So, let's a digital toast to the tour guides of UI design. The icons guide us through the digital world and make our lives just a little bit easier. They may be small, but they pack a big punch. And let's not forget, they're pretty darn cute too.

Now first things first, let's talk about size. I know, I know. Size doesn't matter. But when it comes to icons, size really does matter. You see, icons are like Goldilocks and the Three Bears. They need to be just the right size. Not too big, not too small, but just right. But how do you know what the perfect size is? Well, that's where things get a little tricky.

You see, the perfect size for an icon depends on the screen it's being viewed on. Just like Goldilocks, every screen has its own preferences. A small screen might like its icons a little bit smaller, while a larger screen might prefer them a little bit bigger. And let's not forget about the different resolutions. A screen with a high resolution might like its icons a little bit sharper, while a lower-resolution screen might prefer them a little bit more pixelated. It's like a never-ending game of icon-size roulette.

But don't worry, there are some general guidelines you can follow to make sure your icons are just the right size. For small screens, aim for icons that are around 20-30 pixels in size. For medium screens, aim for icons that are around 40-50 pixels in size. And for large screens, aim for icons that are around 60-70 pixels in size. Of course, these are just guidelines and you'll want to test your icons on different screens to make sure they're the perfect size for each one.

Now, let's talk about the actual design of the icon. This is where things get really fun. You see, icons are like little pieces of art. They're small but mighty, and they have the power to communicate a lot with just a few lines and shapes. But where do you even start when it comes to designing an icon? Well, first things first, you need to understand the message you're trying to communicate. What function does this icon represent? What kind of feeling do you want it to evoke? Once you have a clear understanding of the message, you can start experimenting with different shapes and lines to create an icon that communicates that message in the most effective way possible.

Another important aspect of icon design is consistency. Just like size, consistency is key when it comes to icons. You want to make sure that all of your icons have a similar style and feel. Think of it like a little icon family. They may be different shapes and sizes, but they all belong to the same design family. This will create a sense of familiarity and organization for the user.

And last but not least, don't be afraid to have fun with your icon design. Icons are like little pieces of digital art, so don't be afraid to get creative and play around with different shapes and lines. And remember, the best icons are the ones that are both functional and visually appealing. So, have fun, be creative, and let your inner icon designer shine!

Overall, icons are the travel guides of UI design. They may be small, but they pack a big punch when it comes to navigating the digital world. They're like the ultimate shorthand, helping us process information faster and creating a sense of consistency and organization. And let's not forget, they're pretty darn cute too. But don't be fooled, designing the perfect icon is no easy feat. It's a delicate balance of size, design, and consistency. But with a clear understanding of the message, you're trying to communicate, a little bit of creativity, and a dash of Goldilocks-style experimentation, you can create icons that are just the right size, just the right design, and just the right amount of awesome. So, embrace your inner icon-designer and let your icons guide users through the digital landscape with ease and a little bit of humor.

A Picture Is Worth a Thousand Clicks

Images are the lifeblood of the user experience. Without them, our interfaces would be nothing more than a boring sea of text and buttons. So, let's dive into the importance of images in UI design and why they're like the cherry on the toppings of a pizza, the frosting on a cupcake, the... you get the idea.

First off, let's talk about the power of images. They have the ability to grab our attention and hold it, unlike a block of text that might just blend into the background. Think about it, when you're scrolling through your social media feed, which posts catch your eye first? The ones with vibrant, eye-catching images, of course!

Now, let's talk about the importance of images in UI design. They can help convey information in a clear and concise way, without overwhelming the user with text. For example, if you're designing an app for a restaurant, a photo of a delicious-looking burger can do more to entice a user to order it than a bunch of words describing it.

But images aren't just there to make things look pretty. They also have a functional role in UI design. Take buttons for example. A button with an image of a play icon is much more intuitive than one that just says "play." It's like the difference between a traffic light and a stop sign. Sure, both tell you to stop, but one is much clear and easy to understand.

But what about accessibility? Fear not, my friends. Images can also be used to enhance accessibility in UI design. For example, using alt text to describe an image for users who are visually impaired. It's like the audio description feature on a movie, but for the internet.

Now, let's talk about the importance of choosing the right images for your UI design. It's like putting together an outfit for a fancy event. You want to make sure everything coordinates and looks good together. The same goes for images in UI design. They should complement the overall look and feel of your interface, rather than detract from it.

Images are like the secret ingredient in a recipe for a successful UI design. They add flavor, functionality, and accessibility to the mix. So, remember to choose your images wisely and make sure they're working hard for you, not against you. Just think, without images in UI design, we'd all be stuck staring at a screen full of boring text. And that's just not a world I want to live in.

Now let's talk about using images correctly. I know what you're thinking, "But wait, I thought images were just supposed to make things look pretty?" Well, my dear, you couldn't be more wrong. Images are actually the secret sauce that brings your design to life. They break up the text, add personality, and can even guide the user's journey through your app or website. But like any good recipe, you need to use the right ingredients in the right amount. Too many images can clutter your design and make it hard for the user to focus on what's important. Too few images and your design can feel bland and boring. So, how do you find that perfect balance?

Well, first, you need to know what type of images you're looking for. Are you trying to add a pop of color to your design? Are you trying to showcase your products or services? Or are you trying to create a sense of emotion or mood? Once you know what you're looking for, it's time to start browsing for the perfect image.

How the hell and where do I find these images? Well, there are plenty of places to search. You can start by looking at stock image websites like Shutterstock, Unsplash, and Pexels. They have a wide variety of images to choose from and they're easy to use. Plus, they're all free to use!

But, let's be real, sometimes those stock images can feel a little too generic. So, what if you want something a little more unique? Well, you could always take your own photos or hire a photographer to take them for you. This way, you'll have images that no one else has and they'll perfectly match your brand.

And, let's be honest, not all of us are photographers and not all of us have the budget to hire one. So, what's the next best option? Well, my dear, you can always create your own illustrations or graphics. This way, you'll have something that's completely unique to your brand and you'll have the added bonus of being able to customize it exactly how you want.

Now, that we've covered where to find images, let's talk about where to place them. The placement of an image can make or break your design. So, where should you place them? Well, my dear, that depends on what type of image you're using.

If you're using an image to break up the text, then you'll want to place it in between paragraphs or sections of text. This way, the user's eye can rest on the image for a moment before continuing to read.

If you're using an image to showcase your products or services, then you'll want to place them on your homepage or landing page. This way, the user will be able to see them right away and they'll know what your website is all about.

And if you're using an image to create a sense of emotion or mood, then you'll want to place it in the background of your design. This way, it'll be subtle but still have an impact on the overall feel of your website or app.

And there you have it. The secrets to using images correctly and where to find the best ones. Now, go forth and create beautiful designs! And remember, always use the right number of images and place them in the right spot.

In conclusion, my pixelated friends, the use of images in UI design is not just about making things look pretty. It's about adding personality, guiding the user's journey, and creating a sense of emotion or mood. But, like any good recipe, it's important to use the right amount and place them in the right spot. So, whether you're using stock images, your own photos, illustrations, or graphics, always remember to use them wisely and creatively. And remember, a design without images is like a pizza without cheese, bland and boring. So, go forth and add that extra sprinkle of personality and pizzazz to your designs with the power of images!

Illustrating like a Boss

As any good designer knows, one of the most important elements of a successful UI is the use of illustrations.

But why are illustrations so important, you ask? Well, let me tell you, my dear reader. Illustrations add personality, charm, and a sense of fun to a design. They can also help users understand complex concepts and make the overall experience more engaging and memorable. But before we dive into the nitty-gritty of illustration design, let's first explore the history of illustrations in UI design.

In the early days of the internet, illustrations in UI design were few and far between. Websites were mostly text-based, with the occasional image thrown in for good measure. But as the internet evolved and web design became more sophisticated, illustrations began to play a more prominent role.

One of the early pioneers of illustration in UI design was none other than the king of the internet himself, Al Gore. That's right, folks, you heard me correctly. In the early 2000s, Al Gore's website featured a cartoon version of himself, complete with suit and tie, giving a presentation on the importance of the internet. It was a revolutionary moment in UI design and set the stage for the use of illustrations in web design for years to come.

But it wasn't just Al Gore who was using illustrations in UI design. Other websites, like Myspace and Facebook, also began incorporating illustrations into their designs. But it wasn't until the rise of mobile apps that illustrations really took off.

With the small screens of smartphones and tablets, designers had to find new ways to communicate information and make the overall experience more engaging. And what better way to do that than with illustrations? From cute little icons to full-screen animations, illustrations became a staple of mobile app design.

First and foremost, illustrations add personality to a design. They can make a website or app feel more human and approachable, which is especially important for businesses looking to connect with their customers.

Illustrations can also help users understand complex concepts. For example, imagine you're designing a website for a financial institution. If you use text to explain how a savings account works, it might be a bit dry and boring. But if you use illustrations to show a little piggy bank growing bigger and bigger as the user saves more money, it becomes a lot more engaging and easier to understand.

Finally, illustrations can make the overall experience more memorable. We all know that a picture is worth a thousand words, and the same is true for illustrations in UI design. When users see a cute illustration or a clever animation, it sticks with them and makes the experience more enjoyable.

Are you ready to take your UI design game to the next level? Of course, you are, because you're a boss and you're here to learn some tips and tricks for incorporating illustrations in your designs.

First things first, let's talk about why illustrations are so dang important. They add personality, break up text-heavy pages, and make your designs feel more human and relatable. Plus, they're just plain fun to look at.

Now, let's dive into the nitty gritty of incorporating illustrations into your UI designs.

Tip #1: Choose illustrations that match your brand's style and tone

You don't want to be the person who uses cute cartoon animals in a serious financial application. Make sure your illustrations match the overall style and tone of your brand.

Tip #2: Use illustrations to guide the user's eye

Illustrations can be used to guide the user's eye to important information or call-to-action buttons. Think of them as little arrows pointing the way.

Tip #3: Mix it up with different types of illustrations

Don't be afraid to mix things up and use different types of illustrations in your designs. Vector illustrations, hand-drawn illustrations, and even photographs can all be used to add visual interest and variety.

Tip #4: Keep it simple

When it comes to illustrations, less is often more. Simple, minimal illustrations can be just as effective as more detailed and complex ones.

Tip #5: Have fun with it

The most important thing to remember is to have fun with it. Illustrations are a great way to add personality and playfulness to your designs. So go wild, be creative, and let your illustrations shine.

And there you have it, folks! Incorporating illustrations into your UI designs is a piece of cake with these tips in mind. Just remember to match your brand's style and tone, use illustrations to guide the user's eye, mix it up with different types of illustrations, and keep it simple.

Overall, incorporating illustrations in your UI designs is a no-brainer. They add personality, break up text-heavy pages, and make your designs feel more human and relatable. Plus, they're just plain fun to look at. So, don't be afraid to let your illustrations shine and have some fun with them. Remember, a picture is worth a thousand words, but an illustration is worth a million laughs.

Navigate! Don't Get Lost in the UI Woods

Folks, let me tell you a tale of woe and despair. A story of lost souls wandering aimlessly through a digital waste-land, searching for a glimmer of hope in a sea of confusion. I speak, of course, of the importance of navigation in UI design.

You see, without proper navigation, a website or app is like a labyrinth of doom. Users are trapped, wandering around in circles, never quite sure where they're headed or how to get there. It's like trying to find your way out of a corn maze on a dark and stormy night. Sure, you might stumble upon the exit eventually, but it's going to take a lot of time, effort, and probably a few tears.

On the other hand, a well-designed navigation system is like a roadmap to success. It guides users through the digital landscape with ease, giving them a sense of direction and purpose. It's like having a GPS for your website or app. No more getting lost or feeling frustrated, just smooth sailing from point A to point B.

But wait, there's more! A good navigation system not only helps users find what they're looking for, it also helps them discover new and exciting things they never knew existed. Think of it like a treasure map leading to hidden gems. Who knows what riches you'll uncover when you have a navigation system that's on point?

So, the next time you're designing a website or app, remember the importance of navigation. Don't leave your users stranded in a digital wilderness. Give them a map and let them explore the world of your creation. They'll thank you for it, trust me.

Imagine you're at a fancy dinner party, trying to make your way through a labyrinth of rooms and corridors, trying to find the kitchen where the cake is. Now, imagine the same scenario but with a map in hand and clear signs pointing you in the right direction. The second scenario is much less stressful, right? The same goes for your app or website. Navigation is like a map that guides your users through the various pages and features of your app or website.

Now, let's get down to business and discuss some techniques for designing the perfect navigation.

Keep it simple, silly

The first and most important rule of navigation design is to keep it simple. Your navigation should be easy to understand and use. Think of it like a street map. You don't want your users to get lost in a maze of streets, do you? No, you want them to be able to find their way to their destination with ease. The same goes for your app or website. Keep your navigation simple and straightforward.

Be consistent

Consistency is key when it comes to navigation design. Your navigation should be consistent across all pages and features of your app or website. This means that the navigation should be in the same place on every page and should function in the same way. Think of it like a GPS. You don't want your GPS to change the way it works every time you turn a corner, do you? No, you want it to be consistent so that you can focus on driving instead of trying to figure out how to use the GPS.

Make it visible

Your navigation should be visible at all times. This means that it should be easily accessible and always visible on the screen. Think of it like a life jacket. You don't want to be in a situation where you can't find your life jacket when you need it, do you? No, you want it to be visible and easily accessible at all times. The same goes for your navigation. Make sure it's visible and easily accessible at all times.

Make it intuitive

Your navigation should be intuitive. This means that it should be easy to understand and use without the need for instructions. Think of it like a light switch. You don't want to have to read instructions on how to turn on a light, do you? No, you want it to be intuitive so that you can turn on the light without thinking about it. The same goes for your navigation. Make sure it's intuitive and easy to use without the need for instructions.

Make it fun

Last but not least, make your navigation fun. This means that it should be interactive and engaging. Think of it like a game. You don't want to play a boring game, do you? No, you want it to be fun and engaging. The same goes for your navigation. Make it fun and engaging for your users.

In the end, navigation is like a compass in the vast ocean of the internet. Without it, your users will be lost in a sea of confusion and frustration. But with well-designed navigation, your users will sail smoothly through the various pages and features of your app or website, arriving at their destination with ease and satisfaction. So, to all, you UI designers out there, remember to keep it simple, consistent, visible, intuitive, and fun. And always remember, good navigation is like a good map - it gets you where you need to go without getting lost in the process.

21

FOR YOUR EYES ONLY

Keep it simple, silly, that's the true mark of class!

You see, when it comes to designing a user interface, it's easy to get caught up in the big, flashy stuff. But let me tell you, it's the little things that really make or break a design.

Think about it like this: have you ever been to a fancy restaurant and had a dish that looked absolutely stunning, but once you dug in, you realized it was missing that one crucial ingredient that made it taste just a little bit off? That's what happens when you neglect the small details in UI design.

But don't just take my word for it, let me give you some examples. Imagine you're designing a login page. You've got your fancy background image, your big, bold login button, and your sleek input fields. But wait, what's this? The input fields don't have a clear label telling the user what to put in them. That's a recipe for disaster. A user might put in their email address in the password field, or worse, give up trying to log in altogether. So, what's the solution? Simple, add a clear label above or next to the input field. And voila! You've just avoided a major usability failure.

Now, let's talk about buttons. We all know how important buttons are in UI design, they're the gateway to all the good stuff. But what happens when you have a button that's just a little too small? Or a button that's hard to spot because it blends in with the background? That's right, users will be clicking all over the place trying to find it, and they'll probably give up in frustration. So, what's the solution? Make sure your buttons are big enough to be easily clicked and make sure they stand out from the background. And once again, you've avoided a major usability failure.

And let's not forget about spacing. Spacing, my friends, is the secret sauce of UI design. It's what separates the good designs from great designs. A design with proper spacing is like a well-organized closet, everything has its place and it's easy to find what you're looking for. But a design with poor spacing is like a hoarder's closet, it's cluttered and overwhelming. So, what's the solution? Make sure you have enough space between elements to create a clear hierarchy and make it easy for users to find what they're looking for.

Overall, small elements and details may seem insignificant, but they play a crucial role in the overall success of a design. Don't be like that fancy restaurant with a dish that's missing that one crucial ingredient, make sure to pay attention to the little things. And remember, design is all about the details, so don't skimp on the small stuff. Now let's look over those small details.

Navigating the Navbar

Now, I know some of you might be thinking, "But wait, isn't a navbar just a boring old menu that sits at the top of a website?" Well, my dear friends, that couldn't be further from the truth. Navbars are like the glitter of the UI design world - they may seem small and insignificant, but they add a whole lotta sparkle to the overall design.

First things first, let's break down the word "navbar." It's a combination of "navigation" and "bar," which is pretty self-explanatory. It's a bar that helps you navigate through a website. But why do we need a special bar for that? Can't we just use the back button on our browser or click on the links in the footer? Well, my friends, that's like trying to make a sandwich with just bread and bread - it's not gonna work. Navbars are like the lettuce and tomato of the website - they add structure and organization to the overall design.

Navbars are especially important in today's world of websites with a million pages. Think of it like a mall - you don't want to be wandering aimlessly through the stores, trying to find the one you want. You want a map, or better yet, a directory that tells you exactly where everything is. That's what a navbar does for a website. It's like a directory of all the pages, so you don't have to wander aimlessly through the internet, getting lost in a sea of links.

But here's the thing - navbars aren't just a boring old list of links. They can be so much more. They can be interactive, with dropdown menus and hover effects. They can be responsive, changing depending on the size of the screen. They can be colorful and bold, adding a splash of personality to the website.

And let's not forget about mobile navigation. You know when you're scrolling through your phone and you accidentally click on a link because your fingers are too big? Navbars on mobile websites can save the day by providing a hamburger menu (you know, that little icon with three lines) that opens up a menu of all the pages. It's like having a mini-navbar in your pocket.

Let's be real, designing a navbar can be a real pain in the rear. That's why I'm here to help you design the perfect navbar and make it a breeze. First things first, let's talk about the basics of navbar design. A navbar should be simple, easy to use, and easy to read. It should also be consistent across all pages of your website. This means that the font, colors, and layout should be the same on every page. This will make it easier for your users to navigate and will also make your website look more professional.

Now, let's talk about the layout of your navbar. The most important thing to remember is that the navbar should be at the top of the page. This is where most people expect to find it and it makes it easy for them to access it. You should also make sure that the navbar is visible on all pages of your website. This means that it should be at the top of the page even when the user is scrolling down.

When it comes to the actual design of the navbar, it's important to keep it simple. You should use a font that is easy to read and you should keep the number of items in the navbar to a minimum. This will make it easier for your users to find what they're looking for and will also make your website look more professional.

Now, let's talk about the colors of your navbar. You should use colors that are consistent with the rest of your website. This means that you should use the same colors for the navbar as you do for the rest of your website. This will make it easy for your users to recognize the navbar and will also make your website look more professional.

Finally, let's talk about the functionality of your navbar. The most important thing to remember is that the navbar should be easy to use. This means that it should be easy to click on the items in the navbar and it should also be easy to navigate. You should also make sure that the navbar is responsive, which means that it should work on all devices.

In last, designing a navbar can be a real hoot if you know what you're doing. It's the key to making your website look like a boss. Remember to keep it simple, make it easy to use, and make sure it's consistent across all pages. And most importantly, don't take yourself too seriously. Have fun with it and let your creative juices flow. After all, a good navbar is all about making your users happy. So go forth and design the best navbar the world has ever seen. And remember, a good navbar is like a good dad joke, it's cheesy but you can't help but laugh.

Headers Will Rock You

Those little things at the top of your screens that you probably don't give much thought to. Now, it's time to start giving headers the attention they deserve, because they are the unsung heroes of UI design.

But first, let's define what a header is. A header, in the context of UI design, is the topmost element on a screen that typically contains the title or main navigation for that screen. It's like the head honcho of the screen, the boss man, the big cheese. It's the element that sets the tone for the rest of the screen, and it's the first thing users see when they open your app or website.

Now, you might be thinking, "But wait, can't I just put the title of my screen in the middle or bottom of the screen? What's the big deal about headers?" Well, my dear designer, headers serve a much greater purpose than just displaying the title of the screen. They help to organize and structure the information on the screen, making it easier for users to navigate and understand.

Think of headers as the CEO of your screen. They are responsible for making sure that all the other elements on the screen are working together cohesively and efficiently. Without a strong header, your screen is like a company without a leader, chaos and confusion will ensue.

Headers also play a critical role in creating a consistent visual hierarchy on your screen. By placing the most important information (like the title or main navigation) in the header, you are telling users where to look first and what is the most important information on the screen. This helps to guide users through your app or website, making it easier for them to find what they are looking for and complete their tasks.

But headers aren't just important for functionality and usability, they also play a major role in the overall aesthetic of your design. A well-designed header can make your app or website look polished and professional, while a poorly designed header can make it look sloppy and unrefined. So, if you want to impress your users and make them want to stick around, you better make sure your headers are on point.

First, let's establish some ground rules. Rule number one: No more boring headers. I'm talking plain text, standard font, and zero personality. We're designers, for Pete's sake! Let's start acting like it.

Rule number two: Size does matter. Your header should be big enough to make a statement, but not so big that it takes over the whole page. A good rule of thumb is to make it about 1/3 of the page. Trust me, you'll thank me later.

Rule number three: Use imagery wisely. A well-chosen image can add a lot to a header, but don't get carried away. One image per header is more than enough. Unless, of course, you want to create the world's first header mural, in which case, go for it!

Now that we have the basics down, let's get into the nitty-gritty of header design.

First up, is typography. This is where you can really have some fun. Mix and match fonts, play with size and color, and don't be afraid to get a little wild. Now, I know you may be tempted to use that fancy cursive font you found on dafont.com, but trust me when I say it's not the best choice for headers. Stick with clean, easy-to-read fonts like Arial or Helvetica. And please, for the love of all that is holy, avoid using Comic Sans. It's like wearing crocs to a fancy dinner party - just don't do it. Just make sure it's readable, otherwise, what's the point?

Next, spacing. This is where a lot of designers go wrong. They cram everything into the header, leaving no room to breathe. Give your text and imagery some space, it'll make a world of difference.

Next up, is the all-important hierarchy. Make sure the most important information is front and center, and the less important stuff is tucked away in the corners. It's like a game of Tetris, but with text. And trust me, you don't want to be the designer who lets their header get "game over."

Now, for the grand finale: placement. A header should be placed in a logical and consistent spot, so users know where to find it. It should also be easy to navigate to and from. Don't make your users play a game of hide and seek with your header.

In the massive end, header design in UI is not just about making something that looks good, it's about creating a functional and user-friendly experience. Remember to keep it clear, concise, and legible, choose the right size and color, pick a font that's easy on the eyes, and place it in a logical spot. And most importantly, have fun with it! After all, it's not every day that you get to play around with big, fancy text at the top of a screen. So go forth and create headers that will knock the socks off your users, leave them thoroughly entertained and also let them easily navigate through your website or app.

Cards on the Table

We're gonna talk about one of the most versatile and useful tools in a designer's toolbox: CARDS! Cards are like the duct tape of UI design. They can be used for just about anything, from displaying product information to organizing content in a visually pleasing way. Think of a card as a little container for all of your design elements. It's like a mini website within a website.

Now, you might be wondering, "But why use cards when I can just use plain old divs and spans?" Well, designers, cards come with built-in functionality and style options that make them a designer's dream. Plus, they add an extra layer of organization to your layout, making it easier for users to scan and find the information they're looking for.

But enough with the technical talk, let's get to the fun stuff! Have you ever seen a card that makes you do a double-take? Like, "Wait, is that a card or a piece of fancy origami?" That's the beauty of cards, they can be as simple or as complex as you want them to be.

And let's not forget about the endless possibilities for customization. You can play around with different shapes, sizes, and colors to make your cards truly stand out. Want a card that looks like a postcard from the 1920s? Done. Want a card that looks like a giant fortune cookie? Also done. The possibilities are endless, my friends.

But perhaps the best thing about cards is that they can be used for comedic effects. Imagine a card that looks like a giant "Get Well Soon" card for your friend who's been feeling under the weather. Or a card that looks like a giant game of Go Fish for a digital version of the classic card game. The possibilities are endless!

Launching Card Rockets! Let's talk about the basics of card design. A card is a container that holds information and is often used in a list or grid format. Think of it like a mini billboard for your app or website. It's like a tiny little package of awesomeness that your users will love to open.

Now, before you start designing your card, you need to ask yourself some important questions. Who is your target audience? What information do they need to see on the card? And most importantly, what do you want them to do with that information? Once you have the answers to these questions, you can start designing your card.

Now, let's talk about the layout of your card. The key here is to keep it simple and easy to read. You don't want your users to get lost in a sea of information. Stick to one main image and a few key pieces of information. And remember, less is more.

Next, let's talk about the images on your card. A picture is worth a thousand words, so make sure you choose the right one. It should be relevant to the information on the card and should be visually pleasing. And please, please, please make sure the image is of high quality. No one wants to see a blurry, pixelated image. It's like showing up to a fancy dinner party in your pajamas.

Now, let's talk about the text on your card. Keep it short and sweet. No one wants to read a novel on a card. Stick to the essentials and use a font that is easy to read. And please, please, please make sure there are no typos. It's like showing up to a job interview with spinach in your teeth.

Finally, let's talk about the call-to-action (CTA) on your card. The CTA is the most important part of the card. It's what you want your users to do with the information on the card. So, make sure it's clear and easy to find. And please, please, please make sure it's not hidden in small print at the bottom of the card. It's like trying to find a needle in a haystack.

In conclusion, designing the perfect card in UI design is like baking the perfect cake. It takes a little bit of creativity, a dash of simplicity, and a sprinkle of humor. Remember to keep your target audience in mind, use high-quality images, and make sure your call-to-action is clear and easy to find. And most importantly, have fun with it! Don't be afraid to add a little bit of humor to your card design, it'll make your users smile and that's worth more than any fancy design. So go forth and design the perfect card, my dear UI design enthusiasts, and remember, always keep it simple and sweet, just like a good slice of cake.

Table Manners

Tables, these bad boys are not to be underestimated. They're like the ugly duckling of UI design, but once they're all dressed up and ready to go, they're the belle of the ball.

First things first, let's define what a table is in UI design. It's pretty much exactly what it sounds like - a grid-like layout that organizes information in rows and columns. Think of it like a spreadsheet on steroids. It's a way to present data in an organized, easy-to-digest format.

Now, you might be thinking "I can organize data in a spreadsheet, why do I need a table in my UI?" Well, my dear friend, let me tell you - tables in UI design are like the ultimate wingman. They're there to help present data visually appealingly, making it easy for users to understand and navigate. Plus, they're a great way to show off your data in a way that's easy to understand and interact with.

But that's not all folks! Tables in UI design also come with some fancy bells and whistles. For example, you can add sorting and filtering options, so users can easily find the information they're looking for. Plus, they can be used to create interactive elements like charts and graphs. Talk about a party trick!

But let's not forget the importance of good table design. A poorly designed table is like trying to navigate a maze with a blindfold on. It's confusing, and frustrating and will probably lead to users giving up and going elsewhere. So, when designing tables, make sure they're easy to read and understand, with clear headings and labels. And always, always, always make sure they're mobile-friendly - no one wants to squint at a tiny table on their phone.

But seriously, tables are very important in UI design, they help to organize data and make it more accessible to users. Tables are not only boring but they can also be used to create interactive elements like charts and graphs, which makes them more fun and engaging.

Alright, designers, it's time to learn how to design the perfect table in UI design. And by "perfect," I mean so perfect that your users will be doing backflips and high fiving each other just to use it. So, let's get started with some tips and tricks that will make your table design the envy of all other tables in the UI design world.

First things first, let's talk about size. Now, I know what you're thinking, "Size doesn't matter, it's all about the content." Well, my friends, that may be true in some cases, but when it comes to tables, size is everything. You want your table to be big enough to hold all of the information, but not so big that it takes up the entire screen. A good rule of thumb is to make the table about 60-70% of the screen size. That way, your users will have enough room to see all the important information, but they won't feel like they're stuck in a never-ending spreadsheet.

Next, let's talk about organization. Now, I know some of you may be thinking, "But wait, isn't that what the size is for?" Well, yes, but the organization is a whole different beast. You want your table to be easy to read and understand. That means using clear and simple labels, grouping similar information together, and using colors and icons to help guide the user's eye. And for the love of all things holy, please make sure your table is properly aligned. Nothing screams "amateur" like a table that looks like it was put together by a drunk monkey.

Now, let's talk about interactivity. I know, I know, tables aren't exactly known for being the most interactive elements on a website. But that doesn't mean you can't make them more engaging. Adding hover effects, sorting and filtering options, and even the ability to edit or delete information can make your table feels more like a tool and less like a static piece of information. And let's be real, who doesn't love a good hover effect?

And lastly, let's talk about aesthetics. Now, I know some of you may be thinking, "But wait, isn't that what the organization is for?" Well, yes, but aesthetics is all about making your table look good. And who doesn't want their table to look good? Adding a little bit of color, using different font styles, and even adding a little bit of animation can go a long way in making your table stand out. Just make sure you don't go overboard and make it look like a clown car.

And there you have it, folks! With these tips and tricks, you're well on your way to designing the perfect table in UI design. Remember, size, organization, interactivity, and aesthetics are key. And always remember, if in doubt, add a hover effect.

End of the line, tables are a crucial element in UI design and can make or break the user experience. They allow users to quickly and easily view and interact with large amounts of data, making them an essential tool for any website or app. And let's be real, what's more, satisfying than scrolling through a perfectly organized and aesthetically pleasing table? So, my friends, don't underestimate the power of tables in UI design. They may not be the sexiest element on a website, but they're the backbone that keeps everything running smoothly.

Widget Sorcerer

First off, let's define what a widget is. A widget is a small, reusable element in a user interface that can perform a specific function. Think of them like mini superheroes for your website or app. They can be buttons, sliders, text boxes, you name it. And just like superheroes, they all have different powers.

Now, you might be thinking, "But why do I need widgets? Can't I just design my website without them?" Well, let me ask you this: Would Batman be able to save Gotham without his trusty Batarang? Would Spider-Man be able to swing through the city without his web shooters? The answer is no. Similarly, your website or app needs widgets to function properly and make the user experience as seamless as possible.

But it's not just about functionality, widgets can also add a touch of personality and creativity to your design. Have you ever seen a website with a button that looks like a banana? Or a slider that's shaped like a dinosaur? These are widgets, and they can add a unique and playful element to your design.

But don't just take my word for it, let's look at some examples of widgets in action. Imagine you're on a website trying to book a flight. Without widgets, you would have to manually input all your information, like your departure and arrival cities, dates, and the number of passengers. But with widgets, you can easily select your options from drop-down menus and sliders. It's like having a personal travel agent at your fingertips.

Or let's say you're trying to create a playlist on a music streaming app. Without widgets, you would have to manually search for each song and add them to your playlist one by one. But with widgets, you can easily add songs to your playlist with the click of a button. It's like having a personal DJ at your disposal.

Now my fellow widget enthusiasts! Are you ready to learn the ins and outs of designing the most visually appealing, user-friendly widgets in the land? Well, buckle up, because you're in for a wild ride!

First off, let's talk about the importance of color. Now, I know some of you may be thinking, "But wait, isn't color just a matter of personal preference?" Well, my dear friends, you would be wrong. You see, color is the backbone of any good widget design as I explained in the previous chapters. It can evoke emotions, guide the user's eye, and even im-prove accessibility. But how do we choose the perfect color palette, you ask? Well, let me tell you a little secret - there's a website called "Coolors" that does all the hard work for you. Just hit the spacebar and voila! A beautifully curated color palette appears before your very eyes. It's like magic!

Next up, we have the all-important task of choosing the perfect font. Now, I know some of you may be thinking, "But wait, isn't font just a matter of personal preference?" Well, my dear friends, you would be wrong (again). You see, font is the cherry on top of any good widget design. It can convey a certain tone or style and even improve read-ability. But, how do we choose the perfect font, you ask? Well, you visit good old Google Fonts or a website called "Fontshare" both have a plethora of options to choose from. And the best part? It's free! It's like a font smorgas-bord!

Now, let's talk about the layout of your widgets. The key to a good layout is to keep it simple and easy to understand. The user should be able to find what they're looking for with minimal effort. But how do we achieve this, you ask? Well, let me tell you another little secret - there's a website called "LayoutIt" that allows you to drag and drop differ-ent elements to create the perfect layout. It's like playing with LEGOs, but for grown-ups!

Last, but certainly not least, we have the all-important task of adding animations to your widgets. Now, I know some of you may be thinking, "But wait, isn't animation just a matter of personal preference?" Well, my dear friends, you would be wrong (yet again). You see, the animation is the icing on the cake of any good widget design. It can add a sense of playfulness, guide the user's eye, and even improve accessibility. But, how do we add animations, you ask? Well, let me tell you a super-secret - there's a website called "Animate.css" that has a variety of pre-made animations for you to choose from. All you have to do is add a class and voila! Your widget is now alive! It's like Frankenstein, but for widgets!

Bunch of secrets, isn't it?

And there you have it, folks! With these tips and tricks, you'll be designing widgets that are the envy of all your friends and colleagues. Just remember, keep it simple, use color wisely, choose the perfect font, layout like a pro, and animate like there's no tomorrow. And, most importantly, don't take yourself too seriously. After all, designing widgets is supposed to be fun! So go forth, my friends, and make the most beautiful, user-friendly widgets the world has ever seen. Who knows, you might even win a widget design award and become the next widget-designing sensation! Now go forth and make some widgets, you widget wizard!

Don't step on My Footer

Let's define what exactly we're talking about here. A footer, in the context of UI design, is the section of a website or application that sits at the bottom of the screen and typically contains information such as copyright notices, site navigation, and contact information. Think of it like the appendix of a website - not always necessary, but it sure comes in handy when you need it.

Now, you may be thinking, "But why do I need a footer? Can't I just stick all that information somewhere else on the page?" And to that, we say, sure, you could. But where's the fun in that? Footers are like shoes - they may not be the main attraction, but they add that extra bit of flair that makes the whole experience better. Plus, it's a great way to keep your users from getting lost in the abyss of the internet.

But the importance of footers goes beyond just providing extra information. A well-designed footer can improve the overall user experience by making it easy for users to find what they're looking for and navigate the site. It can also help with SEO by providing links to important pages on your site. Plus, it's a great way to show off your brand and personality.

Now, on to the fun stuff - the design of the footer itself. This is where things can get a little tricky. You want to make sure the footer is noticeable, but not so in your face that it's obnoxious. You want it to be informative, but not over-whelming. It's like trying to balance a giant ball of yarn on the tip of your nose - not impossible, but it takes a bit of skill.

One common mistake in footer design is cramming too much information into a small space. We get it, you want to include everything, but trust us, less is more. Think of it like a buffet - you want to offer a variety of options, but if there's too much, it becomes overwhelming and people end up not knowing what to choose. The same goes for footers - if there's too much going on, users will just scroll right past it.

Another important aspect to keep in mind is consistency. Your footer should match the overall design and aesthetic of your site. It's like wearing mismatched socks - it may not seem like a big deal, but it can be a little jarring to the eye.

Now some ground rules...

First things first, let's talk about the placement of footers. They should be placed at the bottom of the screen, duh! But seriously, it's important to make sure they are not blocking any important information or call to action. And don't even think about trying to sneak them in halfway down the page, that's just plain rude to your users.

Now, onto the content of your footers. This is where things can get a little tricky. Sure, you can include the standard copyright information and links to your social media accounts, but why not have a little fun with it? Add a funny quote or a silly graphic. Make your footer a reflection of your brand's personality. And for the love of all that is holy, please make sure your contact information is easy to find. Nothing is more frustrating than hunting for an email address or phone number.

But perhaps the most important aspect of footer design is mobile optimization. With the rise of mobile browsing, it's crucial to make sure your footer looks just as good on a tiny screen as it does on a big one. This means keeping the design simple and the content concise. And for the love of all that is holy, please make sure your contact information is easy to find. (Yes, I know I just said that, but it bears repeating!)

And lastly, don't be afraid to get a little creative with your footers. Take a cue from famous brands like Airbnb and Spotify, and use your footer to tell a story, or share a fun fact or two. The possibilities are endless!

In conclusion, footers may seem like a small and insignificant part of your UI design, but they play a big role in creating a positive user experience. So, remember, keep them simple, mobile-friendly, and playful, and you'll be sure to leave a lasting impression on your users.

The Sidebar Strikes Back

I am about to blow your minds with the most important aspect of UI design that you never knew you needed: the sidebar.

Now, I know what you're thinking: "A sidebar? That's just a little column on the side of the screen. How important could it possibly be?" Well, my dear designer, let me tell you: it is the secret ingredient to making your website or app not only functional but also the cat's pajamas (or the bee's knees, if you prefer).

First of all, let's define what a sidebar is, for those of you who may be unfamiliar. A sidebar is, quite simply, a column on the side of the screen that typically contains navigation options. Think of it as the VIP section of your website or app. It's where all the cool kids hang out, and where you want your users to go to find what they're looking for.

But why is it so important, you ask? Well, let me tell you. A sidebar is the ultimate navigation tool. It allows users to easily access different sections of your website or app without having to click through multiple pages. It's like having a personal tour guide, but instead of a person, it's a little column on the side of the screen.

Additionally, a sidebar can also be used to showcase important information, such as notifications or user settings. It's like having a little personal assistant, but again, it's a column on the side of the screen. And let's be real, who doesn't love a good personal assistant?

Now, I know what some of you may be thinking: "But won't a sidebar take up valuable screen real estate?" The answer is yes, it will. But that's the point! You want users to be able to find what they're looking for quickly and easily, and a sidebar allows you to do just that. Plus, you can always make it collapsible, so when not in use, it won't take up too much space. It's like having a magic wand, but instead of magic, it's a collapsible column on the side of the screen. And let's be real, who doesn't love a good magic wand?

Alright, buckle up designers, 'cause we're about to design the perfect sidebar!

First things first, let's talk about the importance of a good sidebar. It's like the little black dress of website design - it's versatile, it's classic, and it can make or break your entire website. Plus, it's like the cool aunt of your website - it's not the main event, but it's always there to offer some helpful advice or a quick laugh.

Now, onto the guidelines.

1. Keep it simple, stupid. (KISS, if you will) Your sidebar should be easy to navigate and understand, so don't get too fancy with it. Think of it like a buffet line - you don't want to overwhelm your users with too many options, so just give them the essentials.

2. Size matters. (Wink, wink) Your sidebar should be the right size for your website. Not too big, not too small - just the right amount of real estate to make it useful without taking up too much space.

3. Make it sticky. (No, not like that) Your sidebar should stay in place as the user scrolls down the page. This way, they always have quick access to your navigation or additional content.

4. Get organized. (Like your closet, but for your website) Your sidebar should be organized in a logical manner, with categories and subcategories to make it easy for users to find what they're looking for.

5. Be consistent. (Like your morning coffee) Your sidebar should have a consistent look and feel throughout your website. This will help users quickly recognize and under-stand it.

6. Have fun with it. (Like a kid in a candy store) Your sidebar should reflect your brand and personality. So don't be afraid to get a little playful with it!

And there you have it folks! Follow these guidelines and you'll have a sidebar that's the envy of all the other websites on the block.

Overall, designing a perfect sidebar is like trying to pick the best flavor of ice cream - there are so many options, but ultimately, it comes down to personal preference and what works best for you and your website. But if you follow the guidelines we've discussed, you'll be well on your way to creating a sidebar that's not only functional but also a delight to use. Just remember, keep it simple, size matters, make it sticky, get organized, be consistent, and have fun with it. And don't forget, just like a good scoop of ice cream, a good sidebar is always worth the extra calories (or code, in this case). So go forth and design my little design wizards and witches, and may your sidebars be forever beautiful and functional!

22

—·—

THE FINAL FRONTIER

Sometimes a feeling is all we designers have to go on.

Alright designers, as we have reached the final frontier of this book. But before you start panicking and thinking this is the end of the road, let me assure you that this is not the last chapter. No, no, no. This is simply the final frontier, the point where we will embark on a journey of discovery and enlightenment as we explore the world of UI design.

Are you ready for this? Of course, you are! You've made it this far, so why stop now? Let's dive in and explore the most important pages in UI design.

First up, we have the Home page. This is the first page that users will see when they visit your website, and it's essential that it makes a great first impression. The Home page should be visually appealing, easy to navigate and provide a clear overview of what your website is all about.

Next, we have the About Us page. This page is all about letting your users know who you are, what you do, and why they should trust you. It's a great opportunity to show off your personality and let your users know what makes you special.

The Profile Page is the next important page in UI design. This page is all about the user and their interactions with the website. It's where they can view their personal information, change their settings, and access their account.

The Blog Post Page is also an important page in UI design. This page is where users can view and read blog posts on your website. It's essential that the page is visually pleasing and easy to read, with clear headings and well-formatted text.

The E-commerce Page is another important page in UI design. This page is all about making it easy for users to purchase products or services from your website. It should be visually appealing, easy to navigate, and have clear and concise product descriptions.

The Rental Page is also an important page in UI design. This page is all about making it easy for users to rent products or services from your website. It should be visually pleasing, easy to navigate, and have clear and concise rental information.

The Sign in/Sign up page is also an important page in UI design. This page is all about making it easy for users to create an account or log in to an existing account. It should be visually pleasing, easy to navigate, and have clear and concise instructions.

The Policies Page is also an important page in UI design. This page is all about letting your users know what they can expect from your website and what your policies are. It should be easy to understand and navigate, with clear and concise information.

The Chats & Messages Page is also an important page in UI design. This page is all about making it easy for users to communicate with each other and with you. It should be visually pleasing, easy to navigate, and have clear and concise instructions.

Finally, we have the Categories Page. This page is all about making it easy for users to find what they're looking for on your website. It should be visually pleasing, easy to navigate, and have clear and concise categories.

So, let's dive into this at the speed of Warp 9, and Engage!

Home Sweet Homepage

The home page is the first thing that most people see when they visit a website, and as such, it's often referred to as the "face" of the website. It's the first impression that visitors will have of your site, and first impressions are everything, as they say.

Now, I know what you might be thinking. Isn't a home page just a bunch of boring text and a couple of buttons? What's the big deal?" Well, my friend, that's where you're wrong. A home page can be so much more than just a boring collection of words and buttons. It can be a work of art, a masterpiece of design that will leave visitors in awe.

But why is the home page so important in UI design? Well, for starters, it's the gateway to the rest of the site. Think of it like the front door of a house. Just like a house, a website has many rooms, or pages, that visitors can explore. And just like a front door, the home page is the entry point to the rest of the site. It's the first thing that visitors will see, and it's the first thing that they'll interact with. So, if the home page is poorly designed, visitors might not even bother exploring the rest of the site. They'll just click away and never come back.

But it's not just about keeping visitors on the site. A well-designed home page can also help visitors navigate the site more easily. Think about it like this: if the home page is like a map of the site, then visitors will be able to find what they're looking for more quickly and easily. They won't get lost or confused, and they'll be more likely to stick around.

But here's the thing, a home page isn't just about functionality, it's also about aesthetics. It's about creating a visually pleasing and engaging experience for visitors. Just like how a beautiful front door can make a house more inviting, a beautiful home page can make a website more inviting. A good design can create a sense of trust and credibility in visitors, making them more likely to stick around and explore the site.

And let's not forget about branding. The home page is a great opportunity to showcase the brand of a company or organization. It's the perfect place to include a logo, color scheme, and overall aesthetic that represents the brand. A well-designed home page can make a brand more memorable and recognizable to visitors.

Now it's time for home page design! Where the first impression is everything, and the stakes are high. But fear not, for with a little bit of humor and a whole lot of design know-how, we'll have that home page looking so good, it'll make your mother proud.

Let's start with the basics. A good home page should be clean and easy to navigate. No one likes to be bombarded with a million links and buttons right off the bat. So, take a deep breath and keep it simple. A few key links to your most important pages and a search bar should do the trick.

Next, let's talk about branding. Your home page is the face of your company, so it's important to make sure it accurately represents your brand. Use your company colors, font, and logo prominently, and make sure the overall look and feel are consistent with your brand identity.

But a home page isn't just about looking pretty. It needs to be functional too. Make sure your main call-to-action (CTA) stands out, whether that's a "buy now" button or a "subscribe" button. You want to make it easy for your visitors to take the next step.

Now, let's talk about the elephant in the room: images. A picture is worth a thousand words, they say, but too many pictures on your home page can be overwhelming. So, choose your images wisely. Use high-quality images that are relevant to your brand and your message. And don't be afraid to use videos too, they can be a great way to grab attention and show off your brand's personality.

But what about the content, you ask? Well, it's important to strike a balance between visual appeal and valuable information. A good home page should be able to tell visitors what your company does, what you stand for, and what you can offer them. Keep the language simple and to the point, and use headings and subheadings to guide the visitor through the content.

Finally, don't forget about the mobile experience. With more and more people accessing the internet on their phones, it's crucial to make sure your home page looks and works just as well on a small screen as it does on a big one. So, test, test, and test some more to make sure everything looks and works perfectly.

In the end, designing a home page can be a daunting task, but with a good sense of humor and a bit of creativity grease, you'll have a page that's sure to make visitors say "wow, this is one good-looking homepage". Remember to keep it simple, consistent with your branding, easy to navigate, and above all, make sure it's mobile-friendly. And if all else fails, just remember that the world's most successful websites all had to start somewhere. So, don't be afraid to make mistakes, and most importantly, have fun with it!

Hail, About Us!

Now we will be discussing the all-important About Us page. The About Us page is so much more than just a simple page filled with text and pictures. It's an opportunity to showcase your company's personality, values, and achievements. It's a chance to make a great first impression on potential customers and investors. And let's be real, it's an opportunity to brag about all the amazing things your company has done.

But why is the About Us page so important, you may ask? Well, for starters, it's one of the first pages that potential customers and investors will look at when visiting your website. It's their first chance to get a feel for your company and what it's all about. It's also a great opportunity to establish trust and credibility with your audience. If your About Us page is well-designed and filled with valuable information, it can help to build trust and confidence in your company. It can also help to differentiate your company from your competitors by highlighting what makes your company unique.

Now, I know some of you may be thinking, "But wait, isn't it arrogant to brag about your company on the About Us page?" Well, my friends, there's a fine line between bragging and showcasing. Bragging is all about boasting and exaggerating your accomplishments while showcasing is all about highlighting the achievements of your company in a factual and honest way. And let's be real, who doesn't love a good showcase?

So, how do we go about designing the perfect About Us page? First and foremost, it's important to keep it simple and easy to navigate. Your audience should be able to find the information they're looking for quickly and easily. It's also important to include a mix of text, images, and videos to make the page more engaging and interesting. And, of course, it's essential to highlight the unique values and achievements of your company.

But, what about the actual content of the About Us page? Well, that's where the fun begins. It's important to include information about the history of your company, as well as its mission and values. It's also a great opportunity to showcase your team and the people behind the company. And, of course, it's essential to highlight the achievements and successes of your company. But remember, it's not just about listing facts and figures. It's about telling a story and making your company come alive.

In conclusion, the About Us page is so much more than just a boring page filled with text and pictures. It's an opportunity to showcase your company's personality, values, and achievements. It's a chance to make a great first impression on potential customers and investors. And let's be real, it's an opportunity to brag about all the amazing things your company has done. So, go forth and design the perfect About Us page and make your company look like a boss.

Me, Myself, and Profile Page

Once upon a time, in a far-off land of pixels and code, a great debate raged on. The people of this land, known as UI designers, were divided on a single question: what exactly is a profile page and why is it so darn important?

Some argued that a profile page was nothing more than a digital vanity mirror, a place for users to preen and primp their online presence. Others insisted that it was a crucial tool for building community and fostering connection.

As a designer, I set out on a journey to explore the depths of this great conundrum and uncover the truth about the mysterious and elusive profile page.

First, let's start with the basics. A profile page, in the simplest of terms, is a dedicated page within a website or app that displays information about a particular user. This can include things like their name, profile picture, and brief bio.

But why, you might ask, do we need such a page? Why can't users simply scroll through a list of names and faces like a virtual yearbook?

Well, my dear reader, the answer lies in the power of personalization. A profile page allows users to create a unique, personalized experience within the app or website. It gives them a sense of ownership and investment in the community, encouraging them to engage with other users and create meaningful connections.

But a profile page is not just about self-expression and community building. It also serves a crucial function in terms of user experience (UX) design. A well-designed profile page makes it easy for users to navigate and find the information they need, such as their settings or messages. It also helps to establish a consistent visual language and brand identity throughout the app or website.

But, as with all things in life, balance is key. A profile page should not be so focused on self-expression that it becomes overwhelming or distracting for other users. It should also not be so focused on functionality that it becomes dry and boring. A good profile page strikes a balance between these two elements and creates a cohesive and enjoyable user experience.

As a UI designer, you are constantly faced with the challenge of creating a user-friendly and visually appealing interface for various platforms and applications. But none is quite as tricky as the elusive profile page. Why, you ask? Because the profile page is all about one person and one person only: the user. And let's be real, most of us are at least a little bit narcissistic. We want to show off our best selves, our accomplishments, our interests, and our personality. So how do we, as designers, cater to this need for self-expression while still creating a user-friendly and visually pleasing experience?

First things first, let's talk about the basics. Your profile page should be easy to navigate and understand. The user should be able to find what they're looking for quickly and easily. This means that your layout should be clear and consistent, with a clear hierarchy of information. The user's name and profile picture should be prominently displayed, and it should be easy to find links to their posts, photos, and other content.

Next, let's talk about aesthetics. The profile page is all about self-expression, so it's important to give the user the freedom to customize their page to their liking. This could mean allowing them to choose from different color schemes, backgrounds, or layouts. It could also mean giving them the option to upload a personal photo or background image. The key is to give the user a sense of ownership and control over their page.

But what about the content? This is where it gets tricky. The user's profile page should be a reflection of their personality and interests, but it should also be curated to a certain degree. You don't want to overwhelm the user with too much information or clutter. Instead, focus on the most important and relevant information and present it in an engaging and visually appealing way.

Now, let's talk about the social aspect of the profile page. The profile page is not just about the user, it's also about the user's connections and interactions with others. This means that the profile page should include features that allow the user to connect with friends, follow other users, and interact with content. This could include a comment section, a "like" button, or even a direct messaging feature.

Finally, let's talk about the future. The profile page is not a static entity, it's constantly evolving and changing as the user adds new content and interacts with others. As a designer, it's important to keep this in mind and design a page that is flexible and adaptable to the user's changing needs.

Overall, designing the perfect profile page is not an easy task. It's a delicate balance between self-expression and user-friendliness, aesthetics and functionality, and content and social interaction. But by keeping these key elements in mind and giving the user a sense of ownership and control, you can create a profile page that truly reflects the user's best self.

The Blogging Game

Isn't a blog post page just a page where someone writes about their thoughts and feelings on the internet?" Well, my designers, you're not entirely wrong. But there's so much more to it than that.

A blog post page in UI design is a page that displays a single blog post on a website. It's the page that users land on after clicking on a link to a specific post from the homepage or archive page. And let me tell you, it's a big deal.

You see, a blog post page is where the magic happens. It's where users come to read, engage, and interact with the content on the website. It's where they can leave comments, share the post on social media, and even subscribe to the blog. And it's all thanks to UI design.

UI design is the art of making sure that the blog post page is easy to navigate, visually appealing, and user-friendly. It's about making sure that the post is easy to read and that the important information is easy to find. It's about making sure that the user experience is seamless and enjoyable.

But why is all of this so important? Well, it's simple. A well-designed blog post page can mean the difference between a user staying on the website for just a few seconds or for several minutes. It can mean the difference between a user leaving a comment or not. And it can even mean the difference between a user subscribing to the blog or not.

In other words, a well-designed blog post page can greatly impact the success of a website. It can increase traffic, engagement, and even revenue. So, you see, it's not just a simple page where someone writes their thoughts and feelings on the internet. It's so much more than that.

But don't just take my word for it. Go out there and explore the world of UI design and see for yourself the importance of the blog post page. And remember, always keep it visually appealing, user-friendly, and easy to navigate. And always remember to make it a little bit funny and interesting, that's what makes a good blog post page in UI design!

Let's warp deep into the art and science of designing the perfect blog post page, complete with all the guidelines and best practices you need to know to make your blog stand out.

First things first, let's talk about the layout of your blog post page. A clean and simple layout is key to making your blog easy to read and navigate. This means using clear and consistent typography, with headings and subheadings that are easy to scan and read. You should also make sure to use plenty of white space to break up your text and make it more visually appealing.

Next, let's talk about images. Images are a great way to add visual interest to your blog post, and they can also help to break up large blocks of text. However, it's important to use images that are relevant to your content and that are high-quality. Avoid using stock photos or low-resolution images that look pixelated or blurry. Instead, invest in professional photography or use your own high-quality images.

Buttons are another essential element of blog post design. They should be placed prominently on your blog post to make it easy for readers to take action. For example, you might include a "read more" button that takes readers to another related blog post, or a "subscribe" button that allows them to sign up for your newsletter. Be sure to use contrasting colors and clear language to make your buttons stand out.

Next, let's talk about the sidebar. The sidebar is a great place to add extra information and resources to your blog post. You might include a list of related blog posts, a contact form, or a sign-up form for your newsletter. However, it's important to keep the sidebar clean and uncluttered, as too much information can be overwhelming for readers.

Lastly, let's talk about the footer. The footer is a great place to add links to your social media profiles and other important information about your blog. You might include a list of recent blog posts, a contact form, or a list of your most popular posts. Again, it's important to keep the footer clean and uncluttered so that it doesn't distract from the main content of your blog post.

So, there you have it – the ultimate guide to designing the perfect blog post page. Remember, the key to great blog post design is to keep things simple and visually appealing and to make it easy for readers to take action.

E-Commerce and the Quest for the Perfect Buy

As we embark on our journey into the world of e-commerce and UI design, we can't help but feel a sense of excitement and anticipation. After all, who doesn't love the thrill of browsing through endless pages of products, adding items to our virtual shopping carts, and clicking that all-important "buy" button? But before we dive in and start filling our carts with all manner of gadgets and gizmos, let's take a moment to explore the importance of e-commerce pages in UI design.

First of all, it's important to understand that an e-commerce page is essentially the online equivalent of a brick-and-mortar store. Just as a physical store needs to be well-organized and easy to navigate in order to attract customers, an e-commerce page must be designed in a way that makes it easy for users to find what they're looking for. This means that the layout should be intuitive and easy to follow, with clear labels and categories that make it easy to find the products you're looking for.

But it's not just about organization and navigation. A well-designed e-commerce page should also be visually pleasing and engaging. After all, you want users to enjoy browsing through your products and be inspired to make a purchase. This means that the page should be well-designed, with high-quality images and a consistent color scheme that makes it easy on the eyes.

Of course, an e-commerce page is nothing without its products, and a good UI design should make it easy for users to learn more about the products they're interested in. This means that each product should have a detailed description, multiple high-quality images, and perhaps even a video demonstration. Additionally, it should be easy for users to compare products, read reviews, and add items to their cart.

But perhaps the most important aspect of an e-commerce page is the checkout process. This is the moment of truth, where users will decide whether or not to complete their purchase. A good UI design should make the checkout process as simple and straightforward as possible, with clear labels, easy-to-understand instructions, and minimal distractions.

Designing the perfect online shopping experience for your customers can be a daunting task. But fear not, for I am here to guide you through the process with a few helpful tips, some clever tricks, and, of course, a healthy dose of humor.

First and foremost, it's important to remember that the layout of your e-commerce page should be simple, clean, and easy to navigate. This means that your customers should be able to find what they're looking for without having to sift through a cluttered mess of products and categories. A good rule of thumb is to use a grid layout and keep your product images and descriptions consistent.

Next, make sure to include a search bar on your e-commerce page. Let's be honest, not everyone is going to want to browse through pages and pages of products. Some people just want to find what they're looking for and get out. So, give them what they want and include a search bar that's easy to spot and use. And don't forget to include suggested search terms in case your customers can't spell what they're looking for.

Another important aspect of e-commerce page design is the use of color. Now, I know what you're thinking, "But wait, I thought you said to keep it simple?" And you're right, I did. But that doesn't mean that you can't have a little fun with color. In fact, using color strategically can help to guide your customers through your e-commerce page and make it more visually appealing. Just make sure to keep it consistent and use colors that complement each other.

When it comes to product images, always use high-quality images that are well-lit and in focus. Remember, these images are the first thing that your customers will see when browsing your e-commerce page, so you want to make sure that they're as eye-catching as possible. And don't be afraid to get creative with your product images. Show them in different angles and use lifestyle shots to give your customers a better idea of what the product will look like in real life.

Another important thing to remember when designing your e-commerce page is the importance of white space. Now, I know what you're thinking, "But wait, I thought you said to use color?" And you're right, I did. But that doesn't mean that you should fill every single inch of your e-commerce page with products and text. White space is important because it helps to break up the page and make it more visually appealing. So, don't be afraid to leave a little room for the eye to breathe.

Finally, don't forget about the checkout process. This is the part of the e-commerce experience that can make or break a sale, so you want to make sure that it's as seamless and user-friendly as possible. Use a progress bar to let your customers know where they are in the checkout process, and make sure to include clear calls to action. And, for the love of all that is holy, make sure that your checkout page is secure!

In conclusion, designing the perfect e-commerce page is not an easy task, but with a little bit of know-how, a dash of creativity, and a sense of humor, you can create an online shopping experience that will keep your customers coming back for more. So, go forth, my dear readers, and conquer the world of e-commerce and UI design with these tips and tricks in mind.

Rent and Roll

It's our mission to make sure that users can easily navigate and find the information they need on a website or application. And when it comes to rental pages, the stakes are high. After all, people are looking for a new place to call home, and they want to be able to find the perfect rental as quickly and easily as possible.

But let's be real, designing rental pages can be a bit of a headache. There's so much information to include, from photos and descriptions of the rental property to information about the landlord and contact details. And on top of that, you've got to make sure that everything is easy to find and read, even on a small screen.

It's enough to make a designer want to pull their hair out and move into a yurt on a remote mountain top. But fear not, dear reader, for I have scoured the depths of the internet and have compiled a list of tips and tricks for designing the perfect rental page.

First and foremost, it's important to keep things simple. Don't try to cram too much information onto one page. Instead, break things up into sections and uses clear headings to guide users through the information. This will make it easier for users to find what they're looking for, and it will also make the page less overwhelming to look at.

Next, make sure that the most important information is easy to find. This means that things like the rental price, location, and the number of bedrooms should be prominently displayed on the page. And don't forget to include a clear call to action, such as a "Contact Landlord" button, so that users know how to get in touch with you.

It's also important to include high-quality photos of the rental property. After all, a picture is worth a thousand words, and users will want to see what the place looks like before they decide to contact the landlord. Make sure that the photos are well-lit, in focus, and that they show off the best features of the property.

Another important aspect of rental page design is to make sure that the page is mobile-friendly. A lot of people will be searching for rentals on their smartphones, so it's crucial that the page is easy to read and navigate on a small screen. This means that you'll need to use a responsive design that adjusts to the size of the screen it's being viewed on.

In addition, try to make the page as interactive as possible. It's always great to have a virtual tour of the property or to have a chatbot that can answer questions about the property, this will make the page more engaging and make it easier for users to find the information they need.

Lastly, don't forget to have some fun with it! After all, finding a new place to live is a big deal, and it can be a stressful process. So, try to inject a bit of humor into the page, whether it's through the copy or the design. This will help to put users at ease and make the whole experience a bit more enjoyable.

In the endgame, designing rental pages may seem like a daunting task, but with a bit of planning, attention to detail, and a dash of humor, you can create a page that is not only easy to navigate but also enjoyable to use. And when all is said and done, isn't that what it's all about? Making the search for a new home as painless as possible.

The Login Lullaby

The sign-up/sign-in page. You may be thinking, "But wait, isn't that just a boring old page where I enter my email and password?" You're damn right!

This page is the gatekeeper to your online kingdom. It's the bouncer at the club, the security guard at the museum, and the gate at the amusement park. Without this page, you'd be wandering aimlessly in the digital wilderness, lost and alone. But with it, you'll be granted access to all the wonders of the internet.

But let's not forget the importance of the sign-up aspect of this page. Sure, it may seem like just another step in the process, but think of it like this: without sign-up, you're just a ghost in the machine. A digital nomad without a home. But with sign-up, you become a citizen of the internet, with all the rights and privileges that come with it. You can post on social media, shop online, and even play games. The possibilities are endless.

So, what does a good sign-up/sign-in page look like? Well, for starters, it should be easy to use. No one wants to spend hours trying to figure out how to create an account. It should also be visually pleasing because let's be real, no one wants to sign-up for something that looks like it was made in the 90s. And most importantly, it should be secure. No one wants their personal information to fall into the wrong hands.

But don't just take my word for it, dear reader. Experience the sign-up/sign-in page for yourself. Sign up for that new social media app, create an account for that online shopping site and join the millions of internet citizens around the world. And remember, without the sign-up/sign-in page, you'd just be a digital vagabond. So, thank you, dear sign-up/sign-in page, for making us all internet royalty. And always keep in mind that signing in with "1234" as a password is not a good idea, it's like a gift for hackers.

Now, before you start panicking and wondering if you're in over your head, don't worry! We've got you covered with some solid guidelines and a healthy dose of humor.

First things first, let's talk about the basics. The sign-in and sign-up page should be easy to find and navigate. No one wants to spend hours hunting for the elusive "create account" button, so make sure it's front and center. And while we're on the subject of buttons, let's talk about size. No one likes a tiny, hard-to-find button (unless you're into that sort of thing, in which case, you do you). Make sure your buttons are big and bold, so even the most visually challenged user can find them.

Next up, let's talk about form fields. The sign-in and sign-up pages are all about gathering information, so make sure your form fields are easy to read and understand. No one wants to spend their time trying to decipher hieroglyphics, so use clear and simple language. And speaking of simple, make sure your form fields are easy to fill out. No one wants to spend hours filling out a form that feels like a never-ending questionnaire.

Now, let's talk about aesthetics. The sign-in and sign-up page should be visually appealing and easy on the eyes. No one wants to spend hours staring at an ugly page (unless you're into that sort of thing, in which case, you do you). Use bright colors, fun fonts, and a clean layout to make the page look inviting and easy to use.

Finally, let's talk about security. The sign-in and sign-up pages are all about protecting users' information, so make sure your page is secure. Use encryption and other security measures to keep users' information safe. And speaking of safety, make sure the page is easy to use and navigate. No one wants to spend hours trying to figure out how to log in or create an account.

In conclusion, designing the perfect sign-in and sign-up page is all about making it easy to find, easy to use, visually appealing, and secure. Follow these guidelines, add a little humor, and voila! You've got yourself a sign-in and sign-up page that's sure to make users smile. Now, go forth and create the perfect sign-in and sign-up page. And remember, always keep the user in mind and have fun! After all, designing should be a joyful task, not a boring one.

Policies Scholicies

As I sit here staring at my computer screen, trying to figure out how to write a chapter about the all-important privacy policy page in UI design, I can't help but think about how boring this topic seems. I mean, let's be real, who really wants to read about something as dry and mundane as a privacy policy? But then it hit me, maybe the problem isn't the topic itself, but the way we're approaching it. So, I decided to take a different approach. Instead of writing a dry, boring chapter, I'm going to take you on a comedic journey through the land of UI design and the great privacy policy conundrum.

First of all, let's talk about what a privacy policy page even is. Essentially, it's a page on your website or app that outlines how you collect, use, and protect user data. It's kind of like the fine print on a legal document, but with less legalese and more user-friendly language. And let's be real, who actually reads the fine print on legal documents? No one, that's who. But that's where the importance of a well-designed privacy policy page comes in.

You see, as a UI designer, it's our job to make sure that important information like a privacy policy is not only easy to find but also easy to understand. And let's be real, that's no easy feat. It's like trying to make a kale smoothie taste good. It's just not going to happen. But that's where creativity comes in. As UI designers, we have to get creative and think outside the box to make sure that users not only find the privacy policy page but also actually read it and understand it.

So, how do we do this? Well, one way is by making the privacy policy page a little more interesting. Instead of just listing a bunch of boring text, why not add some fun graphics or animations? Or, instead of just having a static page, why not make it interactive? Maybe users can take a quiz to test their knowledge of the privacy policy, or even play a game to learn about it. I mean, who doesn't love a good game? And let's be real, if we can make a game out of something as boring as a privacy policy, we've truly succeeded as UI designers.

But it's not just about making the privacy policy page more interesting. It's also about making sure that users can easily find it. I mean, what's the point of having a great privacy policy page if no one can find it? That's like having the best cake in the world but hiding it in the back of the fridge. No one is going to find it and it's just going to go to waste. So, as UI designers, we have to make sure that the privacy policy page is prominently displayed and easy to find.

All in all, the great privacy policy conundrum is a tricky one to navigate. But with a little creativity and a lot of user-friendliness, we as UI designers can make sure that users not only find the privacy policy page but also understand it and feel confident in how their data is being used. And isn't that what it's all about? Making sure that users feel safe and secure while using our designs. And if we can do that, then we've truly succeeded as UI designers. And remember, always read the privacy policy before signing up for any online service, or at least, that's what my lawyer tells me to say.

The Art of Designing Chats & Messages Like a Pro

For some, this may seem like a simple and unimportant aspect of the design process, but let me assure you, that the chat and message page is where the magic happens.

You see, the chat and message page is the backbone of any successful app or website. It is the place where users come to connect and communicate with one another, and without it, the entire design would collapse like a house of cards.

But what exactly is a chat and message page, you may ask? Well, my dear, it is a page within the app or website where users can send and receive messages with others, whether it be through text, emojis, or even videos and photos. It's where we as human beings turn to when we're feeling lonely or need to vent to our friends and family.

Now, some may argue that the chat and message page is just a small piece of the puzzle in UI design, but let me tell you, it is a crucial one. Think about it, how many times have you been in the middle of a conversation, and suddenly the app crashes or the messages take forever to load? It's a nightmare, and it's all because of poor design.

That's why the chat and message page is so important. It's not just about making sure the messages load quickly, but also about ensuring the user experience is seamless and enjoyable. The design must be user-friendly, easy to navigate, and visually pleasing.

But it's not just about the design, it's also about the functionality. The chat and message page must be able to handle large amounts of messages, have the ability to block or mute users, and even have the option for end-to-end encryption for privacy.

Now, I know what you may be thinking, "But, it's just a chat and message page, how hard can it be?" Trust me, my dear, it's not as easy as it seems. It takes a team of designers, developers, and even psychologists to ensure the chat and message page is up to par.

So, the next time you're scrolling through your messages, take a moment to appreciate the hard work and dedication that went into designing that page. And to all the designers out there, never underestimate the power and importance of the chat and message page. It may just be a small piece of the puzzle, but it's a crucial one that holds the key to a successful app or website. Don't forget to always be kind and polite to your chats and message partners as they are also human like you, not a Vulcan like Mr. Spock.

It all starts with a dream. A dream of a perfectly designed Chats & Messages page, where users can seamlessly send and receive messages, emojis fly freely, and auto-correct

327

never ruins a joke. But as with any dream, the journey to make it a reality is often filled with obstacles and challenges.

First things first, let's talk about the layout. A cluttered and confusing layout can lead to frustration and a lack of engagement from users. So, it's important to keep things simple and easy to navigate. A clean and organized layout with clearly defined sections for messages and contacts will make for a much more pleasant user experience.

Next, let's talk about aesthetics. A good Chats & Messages page should be visually pleasing and visually appealing. This can be achieved through the use of color and typography. A consistent color scheme and font choice can make a big difference in the overall look and feel of the page.

But what about functionality? A Chats & Messages page is nothing without its core functionality – the ability to send and receive messages. It's important to make sure that this process is as smooth and seamless as possible. This includes features such as read receipts, message delivery notifications, and easy access to previous conversations.

Now, let's talk about the little details that can make a big difference. One of the most important features of a Chats & Messages page is the ability to use emojis. Emojis have become a staple in digital communication, and they can add a lot of personality and emotion to messages. But be careful, too many emojis can be overwhelming and hard to read.

Auto correct is another essential feature, but it can also be a source of frustration. The key is to find a balance between correcting spelling errors and not changing the intended message.

Last but not least, let's talk about group chats. Group chats can be a lot of fun, but they can also be chaotic and over-whelming. To avoid this, it's important to establish clear guidelines for group chats, such as a designated group chat leader, and a limit on the number of people in a group chat.

In conclusion, designing a perfect Chats & Messages page is a journey that requires a balance of layout, aesthetics, func-tionality, and attention to detail. By following these guide-lines, you can create a Chats & Messages page that is not only functional but also visually pleasing and user-friendly. And who knows, it might just make your users' dreams come true.

The Search for the Perfect Category

As a UI designer, I have always been fascinated by the seem-ingly simple task of creating a categories page. It sounds easy enough, right? Just organize all of the products or infor-mation into neat little categories so that users can find what they're looking for with ease. But as I soon learned, it's not quite that straightforward.

The first obstacle I encountered was the question of how to actually categorize things. Do we group products by color? By price? By brand? By function? The options were endless, and I quickly found myself drowning in a sea of possibilities.

But I didn't give up. I knew that the categories page was a crucial part of any UI design, and I was determined to get it right. So, I rolled up my sleeves and dove headfirst into the great categorization conundrum.

After countless hours of research and experimentation, I finally stumbled upon the perfect solution. I decided to group products by function, with subcategories for color and price. This way, users could easily find what they were looking for without getting overwhelmed by too many options.

I was thrilled with my discovery and couldn't wait to implement it in my next project. But just as I was about to pat myself on the back, I realized that there was still one more hurdle to jump. And that was how to make the categories page visually appealing, as well as easy to navigate.

I knew that the categories page needed to be both functional and aesthetically pleasing, so I set to work on creating a design that would accomplish both of these goals. I experimented with different layouts, colors, and typography until I found the perfect combination. The final design featured a clean, modern look with clear, easy-to-read labels.

In the end, I was proud of the categories page I had created. It was functional, easy to navigate, and visually stunning. I knew that users would appreciate the effort I had put into making their experience as seamless as possible.

The categories page may seem like a small part of UI design, but it's a crucial one. It's the first thing users see when they enter a website or app, and it sets the tone for their entire experience. So, if you're a UI designer, remember that the great categorization conundrum is a journey worth taking. With a little creativity and a lot of hard work, you too can create a categories page that will delight and impress users, the importance of the categories page in UI design can't be overstated, it's the first point of contact with the users and it should be easy to navigate and visually appealing. So, as UI designers, we should always strive to put our best foot forward and make the categories page as seamless as possible.

Now first things first, let's talk about the importance of a well-designed categories page. Think of it like a map of a city - without a clear and easy-to-use map, you'll end up wandering aimlessly and getting lost. The same goes for a website - if your categories page is confusing or hard to navigate, users will quickly become frustrated and give up. So, it's essential that we make it as user-friendly as possible.

Now, let's talk about the elements that make up a great categories page. The first thing to consider is the layout. You want to make sure that the categories are clearly visible and easy to find. This means that you should avoid cramming too many categories onto one page, as this will only make things more confusing. Instead, use a simple and clean layout with plenty of white space to make everything easy to read.

Next up, we have the categories themselves. This is where the fun begins! When choosing categories, it's important to think about what your users will be looking for. For example, if you're running an e-commerce website, you'll want to include categories like "Clothing," "Accessories," and "Home Decor." But, don't just stop there! Get creative and think outside the box. For example, you could have a category called "Gifts for the Dog Lover in Your Life" or "Fashion for the Adventure Seeker." The possibilities are endless!

Now, let's talk about how to make these categories stand out. One way to do this is by using eye-catching icons or images. For example, if you have a category called "Outdoor Adventure," you could use an image of a person hiking up a mountain. This will not only make the category more visually appealing, but it will also make it easier for users to find what they're looking for.

Another way to make your categories stand out is by using clear and easy-to-understand labels. This means using simple and straightforward language that everyone can understand. For example, instead of using the label "Outdoor

Adventure," you could use "Hiking & Camping." This will make it clear to users what they can expect to find in that category.

Finally, let's talk about one of the most important aspects of a categories page - accessibility. It's essential that your categories page is accessible to everyone, regardless of their ability. This means using clear and easy-to-read fonts, high-contrast colors, and clear and simple language. It also means making sure that your categories page is usable with keyboard navigation and screen readers.

After all the chips in, designing the perfect categories page is not rocket science. It's all about making sure that everything is clear, easy to use, and accessible to everyone. So, take a deep breath, let your creative juices flow, and have fun designing the categories page of your dreams! And remember, if all else fails, just remember to keep it simple and let the user's guide you.

The Dashboard Survival Kit

"But wait, isn't the Dashboard page just a boring old page filled with boring old information and boring old statistics?" To that, I say, "No, my friends! No!"

The Dashboard page is a magical place, where all the important information about your website or app comes together in one neat little package. It's like the control center of a spaceship, or the brain of a robot, or the...well, you get the idea. It's important. Very important. But that doesn't mean it can't be fun!

First off, let's talk about the layout. A good Dashboard page should be easy on the eyes and easy to navigate. That's why it's always a good idea to include some colorful charts and graphs. Not only do they add a pop of color to the page, but they also make it easy to see all the important information at a glance. Plus, they're just plain fun to look at. Who doesn't love a good pie chart?

But the fun doesn't stop there. The Dashboard page can also include all sorts of widgets and gadgets that make it even more interactive and engaging. For example, you could have a "Most Popular Posts" widget that shows the top-perform-ing blog posts on your website. Or a "Recent Activity" widget that shows the latest user interactions on your app. These widgets not only add a touch of personality to the page but also make it easy to see what's happening on your website or app in real-time.

But perhaps the most important aspect of the Dashboard page is the ability to customize it. Every website or app is different, and every user has different needs. That's why it's important to have the ability to add, remove, or rearrange widgets and gadgets as needed. This way, you can make the

Dashboard page work for you, rather than the other way around.

I am about to impart to you the secret to designing the most perfect dashboard page in all of UI design history. Are you ready?

First and foremost, let's talk about the layout. Now, I know what you're thinking - "But wait, isn't layout the boring part? The part where you just put stuff in boxes and call it a day?" Well, my dear friends, you couldn't be more wrong. The layout is where the magic happens. It's where you decide how your users will interact with your dashboard, and trust me, you don't want to mess that up.

So, let's start with the basics. You want your layout to be clean and simple. No one wants to feel like they're stuck in a maze trying to find their way to the data they need. Keep it simple, and your users will thank you.

Next, let's talk about organization. This is where you get to be a little more creative. You want to group your data in a way that makes sense to your users. And by "makes sense," I mean "grouping it in a way that makes you look like a genius." For example, if you're designing a dashboard for a car dealership, you might want to group all the sales data together, all the inventory data together, and all the service data together. Genius, right?

Now, let's talk about the data itself. This is where you get to have some fun. You want to make sure your data is easy to read and understand. And by "easy to read and understand," I mean "making sure it looks pretty." Use colors, charts, and graphs to make your data pop. And don't be afraid to use emojis. Because let's be real, who doesn't love a good emoji?

But wait, there's more! You also want to make sure your data is up to date. Because nothing says "I don't care" like a dashboard filled with outdated information. So, make sure you have a system in place to keep your data fresh and relevant.

Finally, let's talk about the icing on the cake - the navigation. You want to make sure your users can easily find what they're looking for. And by "easily find," I mean "not getting lost in a sea of buttons and links." Keep your navigation simple and intuitive. And for the love of all that is holy, please don't use dropdown menus. No one likes those.

And there you have it, folks. The secret to designing the perfect dashboard page. Just remember, keep it simple, make it pretty, and don't use dropdown menus. And you, too, can be the designer of the most perfect dashboard page in all of UI design history. But don't take my word for it, give it a try and see for yourself!

23

LIVE LONG AND PROSPER

A design is only effective when both logic and emotion are present.

And so, we have reached the final chapter of our journey through the history and psychology of UI design. It has been a wild ride, filled with twists and turns, ups and downs, and more than a few laughs. But before we bid farewell to our beloved subject, let us take a moment to reflect on all that we have learned.

First, we traveled back in time to the early days of UI design, when it was little more than a twinkle in the eye of a few pioneering computer scientists. We marveled at the clunky, blocky interfaces of yesteryear and chuckled at the quaint notions of what constituted "user-friendly" design.

Next, we delved into the psychology of UI design, exploring the ways in which the human mind interacts with digital interfaces. We learned about the importance of visual hier-archy, the power of color and contrast, and the many ways in which designers can tap into the subconscious desires of their users.

We also discussed some of the most important elements of UI design, such as layout, typography, and navigation. We examined the different types of interfaces, from the print-ing press to the graphical, and explored the ways in which designers can create interfaces that are both intuitive and efficient.

But perhaps the most important lesson we learned through-out this journey is that UI design is not a static discipline. It is constantly evolving and changing, adapting to new tech-nologies and user needs. And as designers, it is our job to stay on top of these changes and to always be pushing the boundaries of what is possible.

So, as we say goodbye to this book and to our journey through the world of UI design, let us remember to keep our eyes open, our minds curious, and our sense of humor intact. After all, as the great philosopher and UI designer Steve Jobs once said, "Design is not just what it looks like and feels like. Design is how it works."

But before we end this journey, let me tell you a little sto-ry, it's about a UI designer who traveled back in time, to the early days of UI design, he was horrified by the clunky, blocky interfaces of yesteryear and laughed at the quaint notions of what constituted "user-friendly" design. But then he met a wise old man who told him "UI design is not a static discipline, it's constantly evolving and changing, adapting to new technologies and user needs. And as designers, it's our job to stay on top of these changes and to always be pushing the boundaries of what is possible."

The UI designer was enlightened and returned back to the present with a new perspective and a fresh approach to UI design. He went on to create some of the most intuitive and user-friendly interfaces the world has ever seen, and he lived happily ever after.

And that, my friends, is the moral of the story. So let us go forth into the world of UI design with open minds, a sense of humor, and a willingness to evolve and adapt. The future is bright, and the possibilities are endless.

To Boldly Go Where No One Has Gone Before!

But before I end, I want to discuss something because I'm just not a designer, I'm a futurist too.

As we approach the end of this century, we are on the cusp of a technological revolution that will change the way we interact with our devices and the world around us. The future of UI design is an exciting and endlessly fascinating topic, filled with endless possibilities and opportunities for creative innovation.

In the next century, we can expect to see a continued emphasis on simplifying and streamlining the user experience. As technology becomes more advanced and more ubiquitous, we will see an increased focus on making it more intuitive and easier to use. This will involve a greater emphasis on natural language processing and voice recognition, as well as the development of more intuitive and responsive interfaces that adapt to the needs and preferences of individual users.

One of the most exciting areas of UI design in the next century will be the integration of virtual and augmented reality technologies. This will allow users to interact with their devices and the world around them in new and exciting ways, creating immersive and interactive experiences that blur the lines between the digital and physical worlds.

We will also see a greater emphasis on using data and analytics to inform and improve the user experience. This will involve using data to understand user behavior and preferences, and using this information to optimize the interface and improve the overall user experience. This will also involve the use of machine learning and artificial intelligence to create more intelligent and adaptive interfaces that can learn and adapt over time.

Another area of UI design that will see significant growth in the next century is the development of more personalized and adaptive interfaces. This will involve using data and machine learning to create interfaces that are tailored to the unique needs and preferences of individual users, and that can adapt and change over time as the user's needs and preferences evolve.

Of course, as with any technological revolution, there will also be challenges and obstacles to overcome. One of the biggest challenges will be ensuring that the interfaces we create are inclusive and accessible to all users, regardless of their abilities or disabilities. This will require a greater focus on accessibility and usability and the development of more inclusive and inclusive design principles.

Another major challenge will be balancing the need for innovation and progress with the need to protect user privacy and security. As we become more dependent on technology, the need to protect users from the risks of data breaches and cyber attacks will become more important than ever.

Despite these challenges, the future of UI design is an incredibly exciting and endlessly fascinating topic, filled with endless possibilities and opportunities for creative innovation. So, let's get ready to embrace this new era of technological progress, and create interfaces that are intuitive, responsive, and truly make our lives better!

But let's be real, the future of UI design is also going to include a lot of people accidentally hitting their smart fridge and ordering groceries at 3am. And let's not forget the hilarity that will ensue when virtual reality interfaces finally become mainstream and we all become a bunch of clumsy, flailing fools trying to navigate our virtual worlds. But hey, it'll all be worth it for the convenience of being able to order pizza with just a thought.

So, to all the UI designers out there, let's get ready to design the future, and make it a funny one! That's it for this book, but our journey in UI design is just beginning.

The Great Smackdown between the Lean and the Mean: Minimalism vs. Brutalism

In the world of UI design, there are two schools of thought: minimalism and brutalism. On one hand, you have the lean and refined minimalists, who believe in clean lines, simple layouts, and a focus on the user's experience. On the other hand, you have the mean and rugged brutalists, who believe in raw textures, bold typography, and a focus on the designer's vision.

And so, the great smackdown was born.

Minimalists and brutalists have been battling it out for years, each side trying to prove that their design philosophy is the superior one. The minimalists argue that their designs are more user-friendly, offering an intuitive and straightforward experience. The brutalists argue that their designs are more unique, offering a bold and memorable experience.

So, who's right?

Well, it depends on who you ask. But let's take a closer look at each side of the argument.

First, let's talk about the minimalists. These designers believe in keeping things simple and clean. They believe that a cluttered interface is confusing and frustrating for the user. Instead, they focus on creating a seamless user experience, with intuitive navigation and a clear visual hierarchy.

But the brutalists, they couldn't be more different. These designers believe in raw textures, bold typography, and a focus on the designer's vision. They believe that a website should be a reflection of the designer's style and creativity. They believe that a website should be memorable and stand out from the crowd.

So, which side is right? Well, the answer is that there is no right answer. It all depends on the project and the audience.

If you're designing a website for a financial institution, then a minimalist approach might be more appropriate. The user is looking for a clean and straightforward experience, and they don't want to be bombarded with flashy graphics and bold typography.

But if you're designing a website for an art gallery, then a brutalist approach might be more appropriate. The user is looking for a unique and memorable experience, and they want to be inspired by the designer's vision.

In the end, the great smackdown between the lean and the mean in UI design is a never-ending battle. Both minimalism and brutalism have their own strengths and weaknesses, and it's up to the designer to decide which approach is best for the project at hand. But one thing is for sure, both sides are sure to bring their A-game, making for a hilarious and entertaining battle for years to come!

It's All About Logic

As a UI designer, it's important to understand the importance of logic in your designs. After all, you don't want your users to be left scratching their heads trying to figure out how to use your app or website.

But let's be real, sometimes logic can be boring. So, let's take a closer look at why every design should be logical, with a little bit of humor thrown in.

First of all, let's talk about the elephant in the room - users. They're a tricky bunch, aren't they? They like things that are easy to use, but they also like things that are pretty. It's a delicate balance, but that's where logic comes in.

You see, when a design is logical, it makes sense to the user. It's like a game of connect the dots. All the pieces fit together just right, and the end result is a design that is both aesthetically pleasing and functional.

Now, let's talk about the consequences of a design that lacks logic. Picture this: you're trying to use a website, and you're clicking all over the place trying to find what you're looking for. You're starting to get frustrated, and you're thinking, "Why can't I find this?!".

That's the problem with designs that lack logic. They confuse and frustrate users, and before you know it, they're bouncing off your website and never to be seen again.

So, how do you make sure your designs are logical? It's simple, really. Start by thinking about the user. What do they need to accomplish on your website or app? What information do they need to access? Once you have a clear understanding of the user's needs, you can start designing with logic in mind.

Another way to ensure your designs are logical is by using a clear and consistent layout. If your users know where to find what they're looking for, they won't get lost in a sea of buttons and menus.

Lastly, it's important to test your designs. Ask users to try out your app or website and give you feedback. If they're confused or frustrated, you know you need to go back to the drawing board.

In conclusion, every design should be logical. It's not just about making things look pretty, it's about making things easy and intuitive for your users. As Mr. Spock would say "Design must be filled with creativity and happiness, but it should be logical too!"

As always, I wish you a great design journey ahead!

Live Long and Prosper.

BEST DESIGN RESOURCES FOR UX/UI DESIGNERS

Typography

1. Google Fonts

2. Dafont

3. Font Squirrel

4. Urban Fonts

5. Cufon Fonts

6. Font Space

7. Font Bundles

8. Font Fabric

9. Fontshare

10. Pangram Pangram Foundry

11. MyFonts

12. Adobe Fonts

Images & Videos

1. Unsplash

2. Pexels

3. Pixabay

4. Freepik

5. Kaboompics

6. Free Images

7. Burst by Shopify

8. Stockvault

Mockups

1. Mockupworld

2. Unblast

3. Freepik

4. Pixeden

5. Previewed

6. Mockups Design

7. Canva

8. Figma Community

Icons

1. Icons8

2. Iconsax

3. Iconly 2.3

4. IconScout

5. Feather Icons

6. Flaticon

7. The Noun Project

Illustrations

1. Humaaans

2. unDraw

3. Ouch by Icons8

4. Blush

5. Open Doodles

6. Drawkit

Colors

1. Adobe Color

2. Coolors

3. Color Hunt

4. Khroma

5. Muzli Colors

6. Paletton

Inspiration

1. Mobbin

2. Dribbble

3. Behance

4. Awwwards

5. Pinterest

6. Uplabs

7. Siiimple

Design & Prototyping

1. Figma

2. InVision Studio

3. Adobe XD

4. Webflow

5. Editor X

6. Axure RP

7. Origami Studio

8. Justinmind

9. Sketch

10. Fluid UI

11. Framer

12. Marvel

13. Proto.io

14. Principle

15. Balsamiq

A.I. Tools

1. ChattGPT

2. DALL-E

3. MidJourney

Acknowledgments

First and foremost, I want to express my deepest gratitude to the almighty Universe for granting me the strength, wisdom, and creativity to bring my vision of Pixel Land to life.

I am extremely blessed to have the support of my family and friends who have always encouraged me in my endeavors. I want to extend a heartfelt thank you to my husband, who has been my rock and my source of inspiration through every step of this journey. Your unwavering support, love, and patience have been invaluable to me.

I am also grateful to my wonderful team of designers who have helped me to refine my ideas and bring them to life. Your insights and expertise have been instrumental in making Pixel Land a reality.

To my beta readers, I cannot thank you enough for your time, honesty, and constructive feedback. Your suggestions and recommendations have helped me to improve the book and make it the best it can be.

Finally, I would also like to thank my readers for taking the time to read my book. It is because of you that I have had the motivation and drive to continue writing, and I am truly humbled by the love and support you have shown me.

I hope that Pixel Land brings joy and delight to everyone who reads it, and I am forever grateful for all of the love and support I have received throughout this incredible journey. Thank you all, from the bottom of my heart.

References

Don't Make Me Think: A Common Sense Approach to Web Usability *(Steve Krug)*

The Elements of User Experience: User-Centered Design for the Web *(Jesse James Garrett)*

Designing Interfaces: Patterns for Effective Interaction Design *(Jenifer Tidwell)*

The UX Book: Process and Guidelines for Ensuring a Quality User Experience *(Rex Hartson and Pardha Pyla)*

About Face 3: The Essentials of Interaction Design, Alan Cooper *(Robert Reimann, David Cronin, and Chris Noessel)*

Designing Web Interfaces: Principles and Patterns for Rich Interactions *(Bill Scott and Theresa Neil)*

The Design of Everyday Things *(Donald A. Norman)*

Designing Web Navigation: Optimizing the User Experience *(James Kalbach)*

The Web Designer's Idea Book: The Ultimate Guide to Themes *(Trends & Styles in Website Design, Patrick McNeil*)

A Project Guide to UX Design: For User Experience Designers in the Field or in the Making *(Ross Unger and Carolyn Chandler)*

Emotional Design: Why We Love (or Hate) Everyday Things *(Donald A. Norman)*

User-Centered Design Stories: Real-World UCD Case Studies *(Kevin Schneider and Andrew Hinton)*

The Principles of Scientific Management *(Frederick Winslow Taylor)*

Designing for people *(Henry Dreyfuss)*

Walt Disney: The Triumph of the American Imagination *(Neal Gabler)*

Steve Jobs *(Walter Isaacson)*

About the Author

Rahul Raman is a man of many talents. He is a visionary, inventor, and a creative designer. He possesses a deep understanding of design, engineering and physics, and is driven by a desire to make beautiful things, even if no one else appreciates them.

Rahul's approach to his work is unique and inspiring. He believes that fear is a sign that he's headed in the right direction, and it is this fear that propels him to build revolutionary products. He strives for simplicity and clarity in his inventions and designs, and these principles have been the cornerstone of his success as the Founder and CEO of Pexeon.

As a designer, he believes that solving problems through design is a process that can't be fully understood until the problem has been solved. He understands the importance of user experience and design in creating successful products, and recognizes that a deep understanding of the customer is the key to creating a product that exceeds expectations. He believes in teamwork, and knows that it takes a team of talented individuals working together to create a masterpiece.

He also places a high priority on the overall experience of his customers, recognizing that their satisfaction is the ultimate measure of a company's success. He focuses on the larger picture first, putting the needs of people before his own desires, and he always pays close attention to how users interact with his products, rather than listening to critics who may not have a full understanding of his vision.

For Rahul, every great design or product begins with an even better story. He knows that the story of a product is what makes it truly special, and it is this philosophy that has made him the successful and inspiring individual he is today.